St. John Paul II

Y0-BEE-582

# Letter to Families

## The Saint's Reflections on the Grandeur of Marriage and Family Life

With a foreword by
Archbishop Charles J. Chaput

SOPHIA
INSTITUTE
FOR TEACHERS

*Letter to Families* text copyright © 1994 by
Libreria Editrice Vaticana.

Foreword, introduction, and study
questions copyright © 2015 by Sophia Institute.

Cover design: Perceptions Design Studio in collaboration with
Coronation Media. On the cover: "Old paper texture"
(111954803) © Grisha Bruev / Shutterstock.com.

Printed in the United States of America

Sophia Institute for Teachers
Box 5284, Manchester, NH 03108
1-800-888-9344
www.SophiaInstituteforTeachers.org

Sophia Institute for Teachers is a trademark of Sophia Institute.

**Library of Congress Cataloging-in-Publication Data**
TO COME

# Contents

# Foreword

"The family itself is the great mystery of God," a mystery that is misunderstood and even under attack in our day. That is why we so badly need to remember the teaching of St. John Paul II's *Letter to Families*.

This letter came straight from the heart of the great pope. His priestly life was one long testimony to creative fidelity: to his own faithful love for Christ and to Christ's faithful love for every man, woman, and child of our human race.

God's ever-faithful love for his children is the great truth that our secular world has rejected. As John Paul put it, speaking of marriage, "modern rationalism does not tolerate mystery." Ultimately, he was referring to the sacramental character of Christian marriage, to the way in which the union of man and woman in Christ represents the union of Christ and his Church. Yet the phrase can also be applied to the very language of the Scriptures. When God revealed himself to man through the prophets and through his Son, he used everyday human language to make the mysteries of his inner life available to us. Words such as *Father, Son, bridegroom, bride, spouse,* and even *man* and *woman* are of inestimable mystical depth in the pages of the Bible. God knew that by using these words — words that would resonate with the deepest and most heartfelt experiences of his people — he would succeed in giving us a glimpse of the love that is the Trinity.

The irony is that in our distracted twenty-first century we need the testimony of the Bible to remind us what these words mean. It is the Holy Spirit who illuminates our minds through the Scriptures to cast away the darkness of sin and lies about man and woman and to remind us that the most common, ordinary path to human happiness is the path of family life. To the Pharisees who appealed to the Law to justify divorce, Jesus said, "From the beginning it was not so" (Matt. 19:8), reminding them that God created human beings as man and woman as complementary manifestations of his life and love, to join with one another in a permanent friendship of lifelong creative fidelity—a relationship that, since Christ, has been gloriously uplifted by sacramental grace.

Are there challenges to living a life of creative fidelity? Of course there are. But the vision of Christian marriage in St. John Paul II's *Letter to Families* is healing, encouraging, and renewing. Those who read and reflect upon it prayerfully will be blessed with a teaching that will strengthen them for a life of generosity and joy with their spouses, children, and grandchildren.

+ Charles J. Chaput, O.F.M. Cap.
Archbishop of Philadelphia
December 8, 2014
Solemnity of the Immaculate Conception

# Introduction

Catholics today should look to the *Letter to Families* as one of the most precious gifts that St. John Paul II gave to the Church. With so many new contributions to the conversation on the family in the Catholic world, it may seem odd to propose that we reconsider a document now more than twenty years old. Yet it offers a perspective we badly need, for it contains what is arguably the most concise and readable presentation of St. John Paul II's teaching that we must have an accurate anthropology in order to live fully human lives, indeed fully Christian lives.

Over the past several decades, the Catholic Church has articulated a special defense of the family and traditional marriage against mounting opposition from the dominant secular culture. Despite the assiduous work of many, including our popes, the family currently faces an unprecedented onslaught of criticism and abuse. The confusion surrounding the October 2014 Synod on the Family in Rome only confirmed the widespread lack of understanding of the Catholic view of marriage and family, and even of human nature.

The contemporary ideological assaults are made more challenging by the fact that many of our contemporaries —perhaps even 50 percent of North American children today—are growing up in "incomplete families"[1] or as "orphans of living parents."[2] Such has been the case for at least two generations, perhaps more. To defend the Catholic understanding of marriage and family when so many of us lack the experience of an integral family life is a daunting task. Even if many Catholics and other Christians have enjoyed the privilege of a stable marriage and an intact family, we are nonetheless surrounded by a culture that sees, or at least claims to see, the Christian way of family life as abnormal. We have entered a new phase in the relationship of the Catholic Faith

[1] St. John Paul II, *Familiaris Consortio* (1981), no. 77.
[2] St. John Paul II, *Letter to Families*, no. 14.

with human culture, and new methods of engagement are required for the Church to navigate this era successfully.

Consider the difference between our situation and the one that prompted earlier papal statements on the family, such as Leo XIII's *Rerum Novarum* (1891) and Pius XI's *Casti Connubii* (1930). During the height of Western industrialization, the family's chief obstacles were material: the lack of economic resources to provide basic sustenance, education, health, and, even sufficient time for family celebrations, leisure, and Sunday Mass. While there were occasional attacks on the Christian understanding of the family, Western society as a whole nevertheless continued to live by and to accept the basic outlines of Christian family life as their ancestors had done for generations. Very few in Europe or the Americas disagreed with the traditional view that a family was constituted by the permanent and fruitful union of a man and a woman.

Today, however, economic and technological advances have created a society in which more people enjoy physical well-being than ever before, as well as unprecedented opportunities for education and career advancement. The heroic struggles of Catholic leaders to preserve women and children from long hours of factory work now seem almost quaint to us. And yet, paradoxically, in the very societies that have achieved such a laudable measure of social equality and physical well-being, the family, as St. John Paul II observed, is now almost "an unknown reality."[3]

It would be unbalanced to blame the decline of the family on our economic prosperity alone, just as it would be absurd to suggest that further advances should not be sought in order to preserve family life. Although it is true that we should acknowledge and address any and all causes of the declining experience of marriage and family life, what is essential today is to recover the heart of Christian anthropology, the understanding that human beings are a dynamic union of body and soul.[4] The view that body and soul are entirely divided and separate is now dominant in contemporary culture, and it leads to further misunderstandings.

It seems evident that this darkening of the contemporary mind is most profound in the case of sexuality.

[3] St. John Paul II, *Letter to Families*, no. 19.
[4] Cf. Ibid.

# Introduction

After all, most disagreements with the Church's teaching on marriage and family have to do with sexual intimacy. When people no longer understand that the body is animated — literally brought to life — by the soul, they quickly come to view the body as a tool for pleasure and utility. The resulting concept of sexual freedom is nothing less than doing whatever the individual happens to desire. Instead of sexuality being first and foremost the communication of love — that is, the relating of persons who are conjoined body and soul — it is now viewed as a mere interplay of bodies. Not infrequently, this debased view of sexuality becomes centered on one's own longings rather than on the good of the other. And when the spousal aspect is forgotten, it cannot fail to follow that any children who may come to exist as a result of the physical union will also be forgotten. In fact, the idea of procreation has become so divorced from sex that people frequently now express surprise when a pregnancy results from physical intimacy. We are, indeed, increasingly afflicted by an astonishing blindness to the most basic causal rhythm of the natural world.

As sex goes, so goes the family. For when our most natural and intimate way of relating interpersonally becomes limited by a stunted human experience, so do the relationships and family structures that would naturally surround and flow from that experience of relationship. It is unlikely, to say the least, that healthy family life will be recovered without our first having restored a healthy understanding of human sexuality. And in order for us to do that, much will need to be done to recover the common truth that we are more than just our bodies, that each of us is indeed a body and soul marvelously and mysteriously united.

The stakes are high. The fact that God chose the family as the place in which to reveal himself indicates the critical role that the family plays in the divine drama. It is here that he taught us how to be obedient to the Father. In the family, all of us—even God, who made himself obedient—learn what it means to be human, which is also to be made in the image and likeness of God. Most of us can point to experiences, our own or those of others, in which serious family dysfunction has impeded human development. That we perceive and understand these deficits indicates at a most basic level that we expect more from the family. We expect it to be the safe place for a child that the Holy Family was for God made man.

# Introduction

We have tremendous work to do, as Christians and as citizens of modern society, to restore both the right understanding and the experience of an integral, healthy, and happy family life. Thanks to its clear and persuasive teaching, St. John Paul II's *Letter to Families* can be our charter for this work.

Pia de Solenni, STD
Associate Dean
Augustine Institute,
Orange County Campus

# Letter to Families

## From Pope John Paul II

### Gratissimam Sane

1994 — Year of the Family

*Dear Families!*

1. The celebration of the Year of the Family gives me a welcome opportunity to knock at the door of your home, eager to greet you with deep affection and to spend time with you. I do so by this Letter, taking as my point of departure the words of the Encyclical *Redemptor Hominis*, published in the first days of my ministry as the Successor of Peter. There I wrote that *man is the way of the Church.*

   With these words I wanted first of all to evoke the many paths along which man walks, and at the same time to emphasize how deeply the Church desires to stand at his side as he follows the paths of his earthly life. The Church shares in the joys and hopes, the sorrows and anxieties of people's daily pilgrimage, firmly convinced that it was Christ himself who set her on all these paths. Christ entrusted man to the Church; he entrusted man to her as the "way" of her mission and her ministry.

*The family — way of the Church*

2. Among these many paths, *the family is the first and the most important*. It is a path common to all, yet one which is particular, unique and unrepeatable, just as every individual is unrepeatable; it is a path from which man cannot withdraw. Indeed, a person normally comes into the world within a family, and can be said to owe to the family the very fact of his existing as an individual. When he has no family, the person coming into the world develops an anguished sense of pain and loss, one which will subsequently burden his whole life. The Church draws near with loving concern to all who experience situations such as these, for she knows well the fundamental role which the family is called upon to play. Furthermore, she knows that *a person goes forth from the family in order to realize in a new family unit his particular vocation in life*.

# Introduction

Even if someone chooses to remain single, the family continues to be, as it were, his existential horizon, that fundamental community in which the whole network of social relations is grounded, from the closest and most immediate to the most distant. Do we not often speak of the "human family" when referring to all the people living in the world?

The family has its origin in that same love with which the Creator embraces the created world, as was already expressed "in the beginning", in the *Book of Genesis* (1:1). In the Gospel Jesus offers a supreme confirmation: "God so loved the world that he gave his only Son" (*Jn* 3:16). The *only-begotten Son*, of one substance with the Father, "*God from God* and Light from Light", *entered into human history through the family*: "For by his incarnation the Son of God united himself in a certain way with every man. He laboured with human hands ... and loved with a human heart. Born of Mary the Virgin, he truly became one of us and, except for sin, was like us in every respect". If in fact Christ "fully discloses man to himself", he does so beginning with the family in which he chose to be born and to grow up. We know that the Redeemer spent most of his life in the obscurity of Nazareth, "obedient" (*Lk*

2:51) as the "Son of Man" to Mary his Mother, and to Joseph the carpenter. Is this filial "obedience" of Christ not already the first expression of that obedience to the Father "unto death" (*Phil* 2:8), whereby he redeemed the world?

*The divine mystery of the Incarnation of the Word thus has an intimate connection with the human family.* Not only with one family, that of Nazareth, but in some way with every family, analogously to what the Second Vatican Council says about the Son of God, who in the Incarnation "united himself in some sense with every man". Following Christ who "came" into the world "to serve" (*Mt* 20:28), the Church considers serving the family to be one of her essential duties. In this sense both man and the family constitute "the way of the Church."

*The Year of the Family*

3. For these very reasons *the Church joyfully welcomes the decision* of the United Nations Organization *to declare 1994 the International Year of the Family.* This initiative makes it clear how fundamental the question of the family is for the member States of the United Nations. If the Church wishes to take part in this initiative, it is because she herself has been sent by Christ to "all nations" (*Mt* 28:19).

# Introduction

Moreover, this is not the first time the Church has made her own an international initiative of the United Nations. We need but recall, for example, the International Year of Youth in 1985. In this way also the Church makes herself present in the world, fulfilling a desire which was dear to Pope John XXIII, and which inspired the Second Vatican Council's Constitution *Gaudium et Spes*.

On the Feast of the Holy Family in 1993 the whole ecclesial community began the "Year of the Family" as one of the important steps along the path of preparation for the Great Jubilee of the Year 2000, which will mark the end of the second and the beginning of the third Millennium of the Birth of Jesus Christ. This Year ought to direct our thoughts and our hearts towards Nazareth, where it was officially inaugurated this past 26 December at a Solemn Eucharistic Liturgy presided over by the Papal Legate.

Throughout this Year it is important to discover anew the many *signs of the Church's love and concern for the family*, a love and concern expressed from the very beginning of Christianity, when the meaningful term "*domestic church*" was applied to the family. In our own times we have often returned to the phrase "domestic church", which the Council adopted and the sense of which we hope will always remain alive in people's minds. This desire is not lessened by an awareness of the changed conditions of families in today's world. Precisely because of this, there is a continuing relevance to the title chosen by the Council in the Pastoral Constitution *Gaudium et Spes* in order to indicate what the Church should be doing in the present situation: *"Promoting the dignity of marriage and the family"*. Another important reference point after the Council is the 1981 Apostolic Exhortation *Familiaris Consortio*. This text takes into account a vast and complex experience with regard to the family, which among different peoples and countries always and everywhere continues to be the "way of the Church". In a certain sense it becomes all the more so precisely in those places where the family is suffering from internal crises or is exposed to adverse cultural, social and economic influences which threaten its inner unity and strength, and even stand in the way of its very formation.

*Prayer*

4. In this Letter I wish to speak not to families "in the abstract" but *to every particular family in every part of the*

# Introduction

*world*, wherever it is located and whatever the diversity and complexity of its culture and history. The love with which God "loved the world" (*Jn* 3:16), the love with which Christ loved each and every one "to the end" (*Jn* 13:1), makes it possible to address this message to each family, as a living "cell" of the great and universal "family" of mankind. The Father, Creator of the Universe, and the Word Incarnate, the Redeemer of humanity, are the source of this universal openness to all people as brothers and sisters, and they impel us *to embrace them in the prayer* which begins with the tender words: "*Our Father*".

Prayer makes the Son of God present among us: "For where two or three are gathered in my name, I am there among them" (*Mt* 18:20). This *Letter to Families* wishes in the first place to be a prayer to Christ to remain in every human family; an invitation to him, in and through the small family of parents and children, to dwell in the great family of nations, so that together with him all of us can truly say: "Our Father"! Prayer must become the dominant element of the Year of the Family in the Church: prayer by the family, prayer for the family, and prayer with the family.

It is significant that precisely *in and through prayer, man comes to discover in a very simple and yet profound way his own unique subjectivity*: in prayer the human "I" more easily perceives the depth of what it means to be a person. *This is also true of the family*, which is not only the basic "cell" of society, but also possesses a particular subjectivity of its own. This subjectivity finds its first and fundamental confirmation, and is strengthened, precisely when the members of the family meet in the common invocation: "Our Father". Prayer increases the strength and spiritual unity of the family, helping the family to partake of God's own "strength". In the solemn nuptial blessing during the Rite of Marriage, the celebrant calls upon the Lord in these words: "Pour out upon them the grace of the Holy Spirit so that by your love poured into their hearts they will remain faithful in the marriage covenant". This "visitation" of the Holy Spirit gives rise to the inner strength of families, as well as the power capable of uniting them in love and truth.

*Love and concern for all families*

5. May the Year of the Family become a harmonious and universal prayer on the part of all "domestic churches"

and of the whole People of God! May this prayer also reach families in difficulty or danger, lacking confidence or experiencing division, or in situations which *Familiaris Consortio* describes as "irregular". *May all families be able to feel the loving and caring embrace of their brothers and sisters!*

During the Year of the Family, prayer should first of all be an encouraging witness on the part of those families who live out their human and Christian vocation in the communion of the home. How many of them there are in every nation, diocese and parish! With reason it can be said that these families make up "the norm", even admitting the existence of more than a few "irregular situations". And experience shows what an important role is played by a family living in accordance with the moral norm, so that the individual born and raised in it will be able to set out without hesitation on the road of the good, which *is always written in his heart*. Unfortunately various programmes backed by very powerful resources nowadays seem to aim at the breakdown of the family. At times it appears that concerted efforts are being made to present as "normal" and attractive, and even to glamourize, situations which are in fact "irregular". Indeed, they contradict "the truth and love" which should inspire and guide relationships between men and women, thus causing tensions and divisions in families, with grave consequences particularly for children. The moral conscience becomes darkened; what is true, good and beautiful is deformed; and freedom is replaced by what is actually enslavement. In view of all this, how relevant and thought-provoking are the words of the Apostle Paul about the freedom for which Christ has set us free, and the slavery which is caused by sin (cf. *Gal* 5:1)!

It is apparent then how timely and even necessary a Year of the Family is for the Church; how indispensable is *the witness of all families* who live their vocation day by day; how urgent it is *for families to pray* and for that prayer to increase and to spread throughout the world, expressing thanksgiving for love in truth, for "the outpouring of the grace of the Holy Spirit", for the presence among parents and children of Christ the Redeemer and Bridegroom, who "loved us to the end" (cf. *Jn* 13:1). Let us be deeply convinced that this *love is the greatest of all* (cf. *1 Cor* 13:13), and let us believe that it is really capable of triumphing over everything that is not love.

During this year may the prayer of the Church, the prayer of families as "domestic churches", constantly rise up! May it make itself heard first by God and then also by people everywhere, so that they will not succumb to doubt, and all who are wavering because of human weakness will not yield to the tempting glamour of merely apparent goods, like those held out in every temptation.

At Cana in Galilee, where Jesus was invited to a marriage banquet, his Mother, also present, said to the servants: "Do whatever he tells you" (*Jn* 2:5). Now that we have begun our celebration of the Year of the Family, Mary says the same words to us. What Christ tells us, in this particular moment of history, constitutes a forceful call to a great prayer with families and for families. The Virgin Mother invites us to unite ourselves through this prayer to the sentiments of her Son, who loves each and every family. He expressed this love at the very beginning of his mission as Redeemer, with his sanctifying presence at Cana in Galilee, a presence which still continues.

Let us pray for families throughout the world. Let us pray, through Christ, with him and in him, to the Father "from whom every family in heaven and on earth is named" (*Eph* 3:15).

I

# The Civilization of Love

*"Male and female he created them"*

6. The universe, immense and diverse as it is, the world of all living beings, *is inscribed in God's fatherhood, which is its source* (cf. *Eph* 3:14-16). This can be said, of course, on the basis of an analogy, thanks to which we can discern, at the very beginning of the Book of Genesis, the reality of fatherhood and motherhood and consequently of the human family. The interpretative key enabling this discernment is provided by the principle of the "image" and "likeness" of God highlighted by the scriptural text (*Gen* 1:26). God creates by the power of his word: "Let there be ...!" (e.g., *Gen* 1:3). Significantly, in the creation of man this word of God is followed by these other words: *"Let us make man* in our image, after our likeness" (*Gen* 1:26). Before creating man, the

13

Creator withdraws as it were into himself, in order to seek the pattern and inspiration in the mystery of his Being, which is already here disclosed as the divine "We". From this mystery the human being comes forth by an act of creation: *"God created man in his own image, in the image of God he created him; male and female he created them"* (*Gen* 1:27).

God speaks to these newly-created beings and he blesses them: "Be fruitful and multiply, and fill the earth and subdue it" (*Gen* 1:28). The Book of Genesis employs the same expressions used earlier for the creation of other living beings: "multiply". But it is clear that these expressions are being used in an analogous sense. Is there not present here the analogy of begetting and of fatherhood and motherhood, which should be understood in the light of the overall context? No living being on earth except man was created "in the image and likeness of God". Human fatherhood and motherhood, while remaining *biologically similar* to that of other living beings in nature, contain in an essential and unique way a *"likeness" to God* which is the basis of the family as a community of human life, as a community of persons united in love (*communio personarum*).

In the light of the New Testament it is possible to discern how *the primordial model of the family is to be sought in God himself*, in the Trinitarian mystery of his life. The divine "We" is the eternal pattern of the human "we", especially of that "we" formed by the man and the woman created in the divine image and likeness. The words of the Book of Genesis contain that truth about man which is confirmed by the very experience of humanity. Man is created "from the very beginning" as male and female: the life of all humanity —whether of small communities or of society as a whole—is marked by this primordial duality. From it there derive the "masculinity" and the "femininity" of individuals, just as from it every community draws its own unique richness in the mutual fulfilment of persons. This is what seems to be meant by the words of the Book of Genesis: "Male and female he created them" (*Gen* 1:27). Here too we find the first statement of the equal dignity of man and woman: both, in equal measure, are persons. Their constitution, with the specific dignity which derives from it, defines "from the beginning" the qualities of the common good of humanity, in every dimension and circumstance of life. To this common good both man and woman make their specific contribution. Hence one can discover, at the very origins of human society, the qualities of communion and of complementarity.

*The marital covenant*

7. The family has always been considered as the first and basic expression of man's *social nature*. Even today this way of looking at things remains unchanged. Nowadays, however, emphasis tends to be laid on how much the family, as the smallest and most basic human community, owes to the personal contribution of a man and a woman. The family is in fact a community of persons whose proper way of existing and living together is communion: *communio personarum*. Here too, while always acknowledging the absolute transcendence of the Creator with regard to his creatures, we can see the family's ultimate relationship to the divine "We". *Only persons are capable of living "in communion"*. The family originates in a marital communion described by the Second Vatican Council as a "covenant", *in which man and woman "give themselves to each other and accept each other"*.

The Book of Genesis helps us to see this truth when it states, in reference to the establishment of the family through marriage, that "a man leaves his father and his mother and cleaves to his wife, and they become one flesh" (*Gen* 2:24). In the Gospel, Christ, disputing with the Pharisees, quotes these same words and then adds: "So they are no longer two but one flesh. What therefore God has joined together, let not man put asunder" (*Mt* 19:6). In this way, he reveals anew the binding content of a fact which exists "from the beginning" (*Mt* 19:8) and which always preserves this content. If the Master confirms it "now", he does so in order to make clear and unmistakable to all, at the dawn of the New Covenant, the *indissoluble character* of marriage as the *basis of the common good of the family*.

When, in union with the Apostle, we bow our knees before the Father from whom all fatherhood and motherhood is named (cf. *Eph* 3:14-15), we come to realize that parenthood is the event whereby the family, already constituted by the conjugal covenant of marriage, is brought about "in the full and specific sense". *Motherhood necessarily implies fatherhood*, and in turn, *fatherhood necessarily implies motherhood*. This is the result of the duality bestowed by the Creator upon human beings "from the beginning".

I have spoken of two closely related yet not identi-
cal concepts: the concept of "communion" and that of
"community". "*Communion*" has to do with the personal
relationship between the "I" and the "thou". "*Community*"
on the other hand transcends this framework and moves
towards a "society", a "we". The family, as a community
of persons, is thus the first human "society". It arises
whenever there comes into being the conjugal covenant
of marriage, which opens the spouses to a lasting communion of love and of life, and it is brought to comple-
tion in a full and specific way with the procreation of
children: the "communion" of the spouses gives rise to
the "community" of the family. The "community" of
the family is completely pervaded by the very essence
of "communion". On the human level, can there be any
other "*communion*" comparable to that *between a mother
and a child* whom she has carried in her womb and then
brought to birth?

In the family thus constituted there appears a new
unity, in which the relationship "of communion" between the parents attains complete fulfilment. Experience
teaches that this fulfilment represents both a task and a
challenge. The task involves the spouses in living out

their original covenant. *The children* born to them — and here is the challenge — *should consolidate that covenant*, enriching and deepening the conjugal communion of the father and mother. When this does not occur, we need to ask if the selfishness which lurks even in the love of man and woman as a result of the human inclination to evil is not stronger than this love. Married couples need to be well aware of this. From the outset they need to have their hearts and thoughts turned towards the God "from whom every family is named", *so that their fatherhood and motherhood will draw from that source the power to be continually renewed in love.*

Fatherhood and motherhood are themselves a particular proof of love; they make it possible to discover love's extension and original depth. But this does not take place automatically. Rather, it is a task entrusted to both husband and wife. In the life of husband and wife together, fatherhood and motherhood represent such a sublime "novelty" and richness as can only be approached "on one's knees".

Experience teaches that human love, which naturally tends towards fatherhood and motherhood, is sometimes affected by a profound *crisis* and is thus seriously threatened. In such cases, help can be sought at marriage and family counselling centres, where it is possible, among other things, to obtain the assistance of specifically trained psychologists and psychotherapists. At the same time, however, we cannot forget the perennial validity of the words of the Apostle: "I bow my knees before the Father, from whom every family in heaven and on earth is named". Marriage, the Sacrament of Matrimony, is a covenant of persons in love. And *love can be deepened and preserved only by Love*, that Love which is "poured into our hearts through the Holy Spirit which has been given to us" (*Rom* 5:5). During the Year of the Family should our prayer not concentrate on the crucial and decisive moment of the passage from conjugal love to childbearing, and thus to fatherhood and motherhood? Is that not precisely the moment when there is an indispensable need for the "outpouring of the grace of the Holy Spirit" invoked in the liturgical celebration of the Sacrament of Matrimony?

The Apostle, bowing his knees before the Father, asks that the faithful "be *strengthened* with might *through his Spirit in the inner man*" (*Eph* 3:16). This "inner strength" is necessary in all family life, especially at its critical moments, when the love which was expressed in the liturgical rite of marital consent with the words, "I promise to be faithful to you always ... all the days of my life", is put to a difficult test.

*The unity of the two*

8. Only "persons" are capable of saying those words; only they are able to live "in communion" on the basis of a mutual choice which is, or ought to be, fully conscious and free. The Book of Genesis, in speaking of a man who leaves father and mother in order to cleave to his wife (cf. *Gen* 2:24), highlights the *conscious and free choice* which gives rise to marriage, making the son of a family a husband, and the daughter of a family a wife. How can we adequately understand this mutual choice, unless we take into consideration the full truth about the person, who is a rational and free being? The Second Vatican Council, in speaking of the likeness of God, uses extremely significant terms. It refers not only to the divine image and likeness which every human being as such already possesses, but also and primarily to "a certain similarity between the union of the divine persons and the union of God's children in truth and love".

This rich and meaningful formulation first of all confirms what is central to the identity of every man and every woman. This identity consists in the *capacity to live in truth and love*; even more, it consists in the need of truth and love as an essential dimension of the life of the person. Man's need for truth and love opens him both to God and to creatures: it opens him to other people, to life "in communion", and in particular to marriage and to the family. In the words of the Council, the "communion" of persons is drawn in a certain sense from the mystery of the Trinitarian "We", and therefore "conjugal communion" also refers to this mystery. The family, which originates in the love of man and woman, ultimately derives from the mystery of God. This conforms to the innermost being of man and woman, to their innate and authentic dignity as persons.

In marriage man and woman are so firmly united as to become — to use the words of the Book of Genesis — "one flesh" (*Gen* 2:24). Male and female in their physical constitution, the two human subjects, even though physically different, *share equally in the capacity to live "in truth and love"*. This capacity, characteristic of the human being as a person, has at the same time both a spiritual and a bodily dimension. It is also through the body that man and woman are predisposed to form a "communion of persons" in marriage. When they are united by the conjugal covenant in such a way as to become "*one flesh*" (Gen 2:24), their *union* ought to take place "*in truth and love*", and thus express the maturity proper to persons created in the image and likeness of God.

The family which results from this union draws its inner solidity from the covenant between the spouses, which Christ raised to a Sacrament. The family draws its proper character as a community, its traits of "communion", from that fundamental communion of the spouses which is prolonged in their children. "*Will you accept children lovingly from God, and bring them up according to the law of Christ and his Church?*", the celebrant asks during the Rite of Marriage. The answer given by the spouses reflects the most profound truth of the love which unites them. Their unity, however, rather than closing them up in themselves, opens them towards a new life, towards a new person. As parents, they will be capable of giving life to a being like themselves, not only bone of their bones and flesh of their flesh (cf. Gen 2:23), but an image and likeness of God—a person.

When the Church asks "Are you willing?", she is reminding the bride and groom that they stand *before the creative power of God*. They are called to become parents, to cooperate with the Creator in giving life. Cooperating with God to call new human beings into existence means contributing to the transmission of that divine image and likeness of which everyone "born of a woman" is a bearer.

*The genealogy of the person*

9. Through the communion of persons which occurs in marriage, a man and a woman begin a family. Bound up with the family is the genealogy of every individual: *the genealogy of the person*. Human fatherhood and motherhood are rooted in biology, yet at the same time transcend it. The Apostle, with knees bowed "before the Father from whom all fatherhood in heaven and on earth is named", in a certain sense asks us to look at the whole world of living creatures, from the spiritual beings in heaven to the corporeal beings on earth. Every act of begetting finds its primordial model in the fatherhood of God. Nonetheless, in the case of man, this "cosmic" dimension of likeness to God is not sufficient to explain

adequately the relationship of fatherhood and mother-hood. When a new person is born of the conjugal union of the two, he brings with him into the world a particular image and likeness of God himself: *the genealogy of the person is inscribed in the very biology of generation*.

In affirming that the spouses, as parents, cooperate with God the Creator in conceiving and giving birth to a new human being, we are not speaking merely with reference to the laws of biology. Instead, we wish to em-phasize that *God himself is present in human fatherhood and motherhood* quite differently than he is present in all other instances of begetting "on earth". Indeed, God alone is the source of that "image and likeness" which is proper to the human being, as it was received at Creation. Begetting is the continuation of Creation.

And so, both in the conception and in the birth of a new child, parents find themselves face to face with a "great mystery" (cf. *Eph* 5:32). Like his parents, the *new human being is also called* to live as a person; he is called *to a life "in truth and love"*. This call is not only open to what exists in time, but in God it is also open to eternity. This is the dimension of the genealogy of the person which has been revealed definitively by Christ, who casts the light of his Gospel on human life and death and thus on the meaning of the human family.

As the Council affirms, man is "the only creature on earth whom God willed for its own sake". Man's coming into being does not conform to the laws of biology alone, but also, and directly, to God's creative will, which is concerned with the genealogy of the sons and daughters of human families. *God "willed" man from the very beginning, and God "wills" him in every act of conception and every human birth.* God "wills" man as a being similar to himself, as a person. This man, every man, is created by God *"for his own sake"*. That is true of all persons, including those born with sicknesses or disabilities. Inscribed in the personal constitution of every human being is the will of God, who wills that man should be, in a certain sense, an end unto himself. God hands man over to himself, entrusting him both to his family and to society as their responsibility. Parents, in contemplating a new human being, are, or ought to be, fully aware of the fact that God "wills" this individual "for his own sake".

This concise expression is profoundly rich in meaning. From the very moment of conception, and then of birth, the new being is meant *to express fully his humanity*, to "find himself" as a person. This is true for absolutely everyone, including the chronically ill and the disabled. "To be human" is his fundamental vocation: "to be human" in accordance with the gift received, in accordance with that "talent" which is humanity itself, and only then in accordance with other talents. In this sense God wills every man "for his own sake". *In God's plan*, however, the vocation of the human person extends beyond the boundaries of time. It encounters the will of the Father revealed in the Incarnate Word: *God's will is to lavish upon man a sharing in his own divine life*. As Christ says: "I came that they may have life and have it abundantly" (*Jn* 10:10).

Does affirming man's ultimate destiny not conflict with the statement that God wills man "for his own sake"? If he has been created for divine life, can man truly exist "for his own sake"? This is a critical question, one of great significance both for the beginning of his earthly life and its end: it is important for the whole span of his life. It might appear that in destining man for divine life God definitively takes away man's existing "for his own sake". What then is the relationship between the life of the person and his sharing in the life of the Trinity? Saint

Augustine provides us with the answer in his celebrated phrase: "Our heart is restless until it rests in you". This "restless heart" serves to point out that between the one finality and the other there is in fact no contradiction, but rather a relationship, a complementarity, a unity. By his very genealogy, the person created in the image and likeness of God, *exists "for his own sake"* and reaches fulfilment precisely *by sharing in God's life.* The content of this self-fulfilment is the fullness of life in God, proclaimed by Christ (cf. *Jn* 6:37-40), who redeemed us precisely so that we might come to share it (cf. *Mk* 10:45).

It is for themselves that married couples want children; in children they see the crowning of their own love for each other. They want children for the family, as a *priceless gift.* This is quite understandable. Nonetheless, in conjugal love and in paternal and maternal love we should find inscribed the same truth about man which the Council expressed in a clear and concise way in its statement that God "willed man for his own sake". It is thus necessary that the will of the parents should be in harmony with the will of God. *They must want the new human creature in the same way as the Creator wants him:* "for himself". Our human will is always and inevitably subject to the law of time and change. The divine will, on the other hand, is eternal. As we read in the Book of the Prophet Jeremiah: "Before I formed you in the womb I knew you, and before you were born I consecrated you" (*Jer* 1:5). The genealogy of the person is thus united with the eternity of God, and only then with human fatherhood and motherhood, which are realized in time. At the moment of conception itself, man is already destined to eternity in God.

### The common good of marriage and the family

10. Marital consent defines and consolidates *the good common to marriage and to the family*. "I, N., take you, N., to be my wife (husband). I promise to be true to you in good times and in bad, in sickness and in health. I will love you and honour you all the days of my life". Marriage is a unique communion of persons, and it is on the basis of this communion that the family is called to become a community of persons. This is a commitment which the bride and groom undertake "before God and his Church", as the celebrant reminds them before they exchange their consent. Those who take part in the rite are witnesses of this commitment, for in a certain sense they represent

the Church and society, the settings in which the new family will live and grow.

The words of consent define the common good of the *couple and of the family*. First, the common good of the spouses: love, fidelity, honour, the permanence of their union until death — "all the days of my life". The good of both, which is at the same time the good of each, must then become the good of the children. The common good, by its very nature, both unites individual persons and ensures the true good of each. If the Church (and the State for that matter) receives the consent which the spouses express in the words cited above, she does so because that consent is "written in their hearts" (*Rom* 2:15). It is the spouses who give their consent to each other by a solemn promise, that is by confirming the truth of that consent in the sight of God. As baptized Christians, they are the ministers of the Sacrament of Matrimony in the Church. Saint Paul teaches that this mutual commitment of theirs is a "great mystery" (*Eph* 5:32).

The words of consent, then, express what is essential to the common good of the spouses, and *they indicate what ought to be the common good of the future family*. In order to bring this out, the Church asks the spouses if they are prepared to accept the children God grants them and to raise the children as Christians. This question calls to mind the common good of the future family unit, evoking the genealogy of persons which is part of the constitution of marriage and of the family itself. The question about children and their education is profoundly linked to marital consent, with its solemn promise of love, conjugal respect, and fidelity until death. The acceptance and education of children — two of the primary ends of the family — are conditioned by how that commitment will be fulfilled. Fatherhood and motherhood represent a *responsibility which is not simply physical but spiritual in nature;* indeed, through these realities there passes the genealogy of the person, which has its eternal beginning in God and which must lead back to him.

The Year of the Family, as a year of special prayer on the part of families, ought to renew and deepen each family's awareness of these truths. What a wealth of biblical reflections could nourish that prayer! Together with the words of Sacred Scripture, these prayerful reflections should always include the *personal memories of the spouses-parents*, the children and grandchildren. Through the genealogy of persons, conjugal communion *becomes a communion of generations*. The sacramental union of the two spouses, sealed in the covenant which they enter into before God, endures and grows stronger as the generations pass. It must become a union in prayer. But for all this to become clearly apparent during the Year of the Family, prayer needs to become a regular habit in the daily life of each family. Prayer is thanksgiving, praise of God, asking for forgiveness, supplication and invocation. In all of these forms *the prayer of the family has much to say to God*. It also has much to say to others, beginning with the mutual communion of persons joined together by family ties.

The Psalmist asks: "What is man that you keep him in mind?" (*Ps* 8:4). Prayer is the place where, in a very simple way, the creative and fatherly remembrance of God is made manifest: not only man's remembrance of God, but also and especially *God's remembrance of man*. In this way, the prayer of the family as a community can become a place of common and mutual remembrance: the family is in fact a community of generations. In prayer everyone should be present: the living and those who have died, and also those yet to come into the world. Families should pray for all of their members, in view of the good which the family is for each individual and which each individual is for the whole family. Prayer strengthens this good, precisely as the common good of the family. Moreover, it creates this good ever anew. In prayer, the family discovers itself as the first "us", in which each member is "*I*" and "*thou*"; each member is for the others either husband or wife, father or mother, son or daughter, brother or sister, grandparent or grandchild.

Are all the families to which this Letter is addressed like this? Certainly a good number are, but the times in which we are living tend to restrict family units to two generations. Often this is the case because available housing is too limited, especially in large cities. But it is not infrequently due to the belief that having several generations living together interferes with privacy and makes life too difficult. But is this not where the problem really lies? *Families today have too little "human" life*. There is a shortage of people with whom to create and share the common good; and yet that good, by its nature, demands to be created and shared with others: *bonum est diffusivum sui:* "good is diffusive of itself". The more *common* the good, the *more properly one's own* it will also be: mine—yours—ours. This is the logic behind living according to the good, living in truth and charity. If man is able to accept and follow this logic, his life truly becomes a "sincere gift".

*The sincere gift of self*

11. After affirming that man is the only creature on earth which God willed for itself, the Council immediately goes on to say that he cannot *"fully find himself except through a sincere gift of self"*. This might appear to be a contradiction, but in fact it is not. Instead it is the magnificent paradox of human existence: an existence called *to serve the truth in love*. Love causes man to find fulfilment through the sincere gift of self. To love means to give and to receive something which can be neither bought nor sold, but only given freely and mutually.

By its very nature the gift of the person must be lasting and irrevocable. The indissolubility of marriage flows in the first place from the very essence of that gift: *the gift of one person to another person*. This reciprocal giving of self reveals the *spousal nature of love*. In their marital consent the bride and groom call each other by name: *"I . . . take you . . . as my wife (as my husband) and I promise to be true to you . . . for all the days of my life"*. A gift such as this involves an obligation much more serious and profound than anything which might be "purchased" in any way and at any price. Kneeling before the Father, from whom all fatherhood and motherhood come, the future parents come to realize that they have been "redeemed". They have been purchased at great cost, *by the price* of the most sincere gift of all, *the blood of Christ* of which they partake through the Sacrament. The liturgical crowning of the marriage rite is the Eucharist, the sacrifice of that "Body which has been given up" and that "Blood which has been shed", which in a certain way finds expression in the consent of the spouses.

When a man and woman in marriage mutually give and receive each other in the unity of "one flesh", the logic of the sincere gift of self becomes a part of their life. Without this, marriage would be empty; whereas a communion of persons, built on this logic, becomes a communion of parents. When they transmit *life to the child, a new human "thou" becomes a part of the horizon of the "we" of the spouses*, a person whom they will call by a new name: "our son . . . ; our daughter . . .". "I have gotten a man with the help of the Lord" (*Gen* 4:1), says Eve, the first woman of history: a human being, first expected for nine months and then "revealed" to parents, brothers and sisters. The process from conception and growth in the mother's womb to birth makes it possible to create a space within which the new creature can be revealed as a "gift": indeed this is what it is from the very beginning. Could this frail and helpless being, totally dependent upon its parents and completely entrusted to them, be seen in any other way? The newborn child gives itself to its parents by the very fact of its coming into existence. *Its existence is already a gift, the first gift of the Creator to the creature.*

*In the newborn child is realized the common good of the family.* Just as the common good of spouses is fulfilled in conjugal love, ever ready to give and receive new life, so too the common good of the family is fulfilled through that same spousal love, as embodied in the newborn child. Part of the genealogy of the person is the genealogy of the family, preserved for posterity by the annotations in the Church's baptismal registers, even though these are merely the social consequence of the fact that "a man has been born into the world" (cf. *Jn* 16:21).

But is it really true that the new human being is a gift for his parents? A gift for society? Apparently nothing seems to indicate this. On occasion the birth of a child appears to be a simple statistical fact, registered like so many other data in demographic records. It is true that for the parents the birth of a child means more work, new financial burdens and further inconveniences, all of which can lead to the temptation not to want another birth. In some social and cultural contexts this temptation can become very strong. Does this mean that a child is not a gift? That it comes into the world only to take and not to give? These are some of the disturbing questions which men and women today find hard to escape. *A child comes to take up room, when it seems that there is less and less room in the world.* But is it really true that a child brings nothing to the family and society? Is not every child a "particle" of that common good without which human communities break down and risk extinction? Could this ever really be denied? The child becomes a gift to its brothers, sisters, parents and entire family. *Its life becomes a gift for the very people who were givers of life* and who cannot help but feel its presence, its sharing in their life and its contribution to their common good and to that of the community of the family. This truth is obvious in its simplicity and profundity, whatever the complexity and even the possible pathology of the psychological make-up of certain persons. *The common good of the whole of society dwells in man*; he is, as we recalled, "the way of the Church". Man is first of all the "glory of God": "*Gloria Dei vivens homo*", in the celebrated words of Saint Irenaeus, which might also be translated: "the glory of God is for man to be alive". It could be said that here we encounter the loftiest definition of man: *the glory of God is the common good of all that exists*; the common good of the human race.

Yes! *Man is a common good*: a common good of the family and of humanity, of individual groups and of different communities. But there are significant distinctions of degree and modality in this regard. Man is a common good, for example, of the Nation to which he belongs and of the State of which he is a citizen; but in a much more concrete, unique and unrepeatable way he is a common good of his family. He is such not only as an individual who is part of the multitude of humanity, but rather as "*this individual*". God the Creator calls him into existence "for himself"; and in coming into the world he begins, in the family, his "great adventure", the adventure of human life. "This man" has, in every instance, *the right to fulfil himself on the basis of his human dignity.* It is precisely this dignity which establishes a person's place among others, and above all, in the family. The family is indeed—more than any other human reality— the place where an in-dividual can exist "for himself" through the sincere gift of self. This is why it remains a social institution which neither can nor should be replaced: it is the "sanctuary of life".

The fact that a child is being born, that "a child is born into the world" (*Jn* 16:21) is a *paschal sign*. As we read in the Gospel of John, Jesus himself speaks of this to the disciples before his passion and death, comparing their sadness at his departure with the pains of a woman in labour: *"When a woman is in travail she has sorrow* (that is, she suffers), because *her hour* has come; but when she is delivered of the child, she no longer remembers the anguish, for *joy that a child is born into the world"* (*Jn* 16:21). The "hour" of Christ's death (cf. *Jn* 13:1) is compared here to the "hour" of the woman in birthpangs; the birth of a new child fully reflects the victory of life over death brought about by the Lord's Resurrection. This compari-son can provide us with material for reflection. Just as the Resurrection of Christ is the manifestation of *Life* beyond the threshold of death, so too the birth of an infant is a manifestation of life, which is always destined, through Christ, for that *"fullness of life" which is in God himself:* "I came that they may have life, and have it abundantly" (*Jn* 10:10). Here we see revealed the deepest meaning of Saint Irenaeus's expression: *"Gloria Dei vivens homo"*.

It is the Gospel truth concerning the gift of self, without which the person cannot "fully find himself", which makes possible an appreciation of how profoundly this "sincere gift" is rooted in the gift of God, Creator and Redeemer, and in the "grace of the Holy Spirit" which the celebrant during the Rite of Marriage prays will be "poured out" on the spouses. Without such an "outpouring", it would be very difficult to understand all this and to carry it out as man's vocation. Yet how many people understand this intuitively! Many men and women make this truth their own, coming to discern that only in this truth do they encounter "the Truth and the Life" (*Jn* 14:6). *Without this truth, the life of the spouses and of the family will not succeed in attaining a fully human meaning.*

This is why the Church never tires of teaching and of bearing witness to this truth. While certainly showing maternal understanding for the many complex crisis situations in which families are involved, as well as for the moral frailty of every human being, the Church is convinced that she must remain absolutely faithful to the truth about human love. Otherwise she would betray herself. To move away from this saving truth would be to close "the eyes of our hearts" (cf. *Eph* 1:18), which instead should always stay open to the light which the Gospel sheds on human affairs (cf. *2 Tim* 1:10). An awareness of that sincere gift of self whereby man "finds himself" must be constantly renewed and safeguarded in the face of the serious opposition which the Church meets on the part of those who advocate a false civilization of progress. The family always expresses a new dimension of good for mankind, and it thus creates a new responsibility. We are speaking of the *responsibility for that particular common good* in which is included the good of the person, of every member of the family community. While certainly a "difficult" good (*"bonum arduum"*), it is also an attractive one.

*Responsible fatherhood and motherhood*

12. It is now time, in this Letter to Families, to bring up two closely related questions. The first, more general,

concerns the *civilization of love*; the other, more specific, deals with *responsible fatherhood and motherhood*.

We have already said that marriage engenders a particular responsibility for the common good, first of the spouses and then of the family. This common good is constituted by man, by the *worth of the person* and by everything which represents the *measure of his dignity*. This reality is part of man in every social, economic and political system. In the area of marriage and the family, this responsibility becomes, for a variety of reasons, even more "demanding". The Pastoral Constitution *Gaudium et Spes* rightly speaks of "*promoting the dignity of marriage and the family*". The Council sees this "promotion" as a duty incumbent upon both the Church and the State. Nevertheless, in every culture this duty remains primarily that of the persons who, united in marriage, form a particular family. "Responsible fatherhood and motherhood" express a concrete commitment to carry out this duty, which has taken on new characteristics in the contemporary world.

In particular, responsible fatherhood and motherhood directly concern the moment in which a man and a woman, uniting themselves "in one flesh", can become parents. This is a moment of special value both for their interpersonal relationship and for their service to life: they can become parents—father and mother—by communicating life to a new human being. *The two dimensions of conjugal union*, the unitive and the procreative, *cannot be artificially separated* without damaging the deepest truth of the conjugal act itself.

This is the constant teaching of the Church, and the "signs of the times" which we see today are providing new reasons for forcefully reaffirming that teaching. Saint Paul, himself so attentive to the pastoral demands of his day, clearly and firmly indicated the need to be "urgent in season and out of season" (cf. *2 Tim* 4:2), and not to be daunted by the fact that "sound teaching is no longer endured" (cf. *2 Tim* 4:3). His words are well known to those who, with deep insight into the events of the present time, expect that the Church will not only not abandon "sound doctrine", but will proclaim it with renewed vigour, seeking in today's "signs of the times" the incentive and insights which can lead to a deeper understanding of her teaching.

Some of these insights can be taken from the very sciences which have evolved from the earlier study of anthropology into *various specialized sciences* such as biology, psychology, sociology and their branches. *In some sense all these sciences revolve around medicine*, which is both a science and an art (*ars medica*), at the service of man's life and health. But the insights in question come first of all from human experience, which, in all its complexity, in some sense both precedes science and follows it.

*Through their own experience spouses come to learn the meaning of responsible fatherhood and motherhood*. They learn it also from the experience of other couples in similar situations and as they become more open to the findings of the various sciences. One could say that "experts" learn in a certain sense from "spouses", so that they in turn will then be in a better position to teach married couples the meaning of responsible procreation and the ways to achieve it.

This subject has been extensively treated in the documents of the Second Vatican Council, the Encyclical *Humanae Vitae*, the "Propositiones" of the 1980 Synod of Bishops, the Apostolic Exhortation *Familiaris Consortio*, and in other statements, up to the Instruction *Donum Vitae* of the Congregation for the Doctrine of the Faith.

The Civilization of Love

The Church both teaches the moral truth about responsible fatherhood and motherhood and *protects it from the erroneous views and tendencies which are widespread today.* Why does the Church continue to do this? Is she unaware of the problems raised by those who counsel her to make concessions in this area and who even attempt to persuade her by undue pressures if not even threats? The Church's Magisterium is often chided for being behind the times and closed to the promptings of the spirit of modern times, and for promoting a course of action which is harmful to humanity, and indeed to the Church herself. By obstinately holding to her own positions, it is said, the Church will end up losing popularity, and more and more believers will turn away from her.

But how can it be maintained that *the Church,* especially the College of Bishops in communion with the Pope, is *insensitive to such grave and pressing questions*? It was precisely these extremely important questions which led Pope Paul VI to publish the Encyclical *Humanae Vitae.* The foundations of the Church's doctrine concerning responsible fatherhood and motherhood are exceptionally broad and secure. *The Council demonstrates this above all in its teaching on man,* when it affirms that he is "the only creature on earth which God willed for itself", and that he cannot "fully find himself except through a sincere gift of himself". This is so because he has been created in the image and likeness of God and redeemed by the only-begotten Son of the Father, who became man for us and for our salvation.

The Second Vatican Council, particularly conscious of the problem of man and his calling, states that the conjugal union, the biblical *"una caro"*, can be understood and fully explained *only by recourse to the values of the "person" and of "gift"*. Every man and every woman fully realizes himself or herself through the sincere gift of self. For spouses, the moment of conjugal union constitutes a very particular expression of this. It is then that a man and woman, in the "truth" of their masculinity and femininity, become a mutual gift to each other. All married life is a gift; but this becomes most evident when the spouses, in giving themselves to each other in love, bring about that encounter which makes them "one flesh" (*Gen* 2:24).

*They then experience a moment of special responsibility*, which is also the result of the procreative potential linked to the conjugal act. At that moment, the spouses can become father and mother, initiating the process of a new human life, which will then develop in the woman's womb. If the wife is the first to realize that she has become a mother, the husband, to whom she has been united in "one flesh", then learns this when she tells him that he has become a father. Both are responsible for their potential and later actual fatherhood and motherhood. The husband cannot fail to acknowledge and accept the result of a decision which has also been his own. He cannot hide behind expressions such as: "I don't know", "I didn't want it", or "you're the one who wanted it". In every case conjugal union involves *the responsibility of the man and of the woman*, a potential responsibility which becomes actual when the circumstances dictate. This is true especially for the man. Although he too is involved in the beginning of the generative process, he is left biologically distant from it; it is within the woman that the process develops. How can the man fail to assume responsibility? The man and the woman must assume together, before themselves and before others, the responsibility for the new life which they have brought into existence.

This conclusion is shared by the human sciences themselves. There is however a need for more in-depth study, analyzing the meaning of the conjugal act in view of the values of the "person" and of the "gift" mentioned above. This is what the Church has done in her constant teaching, and in a particular way at the Second Vatican Council.

In the conjugal act, husband and wife are called to confirm in a responsible way *the mutual gift* of self which they have made to each other in the marriage covenant. The logic of the *total gift of self to the other* involves a potential openness to procreation: in this way the marriage is called to even greater fulfilment as a family. Certainly the mutual gift of husband and wife does not have the begetting of children as its only end, but is in itself a mutual communion of love and of life. *The intimate truth of this gift* must always be *safeguarded*. "Intimate" is not here synonymous with "subjective". Rather, it means essentially in conformity with the objective truth of the man and woman who give themselves. The person can never be considered a means to an end; above all never a means of "pleasure". The person is and must be nothing other than the end of every act. Only then does the action correspond to the true dignity of the person.

In concluding our reflection on this important and sensitive subject, I wish to offer special encouragement above all to you, dear married couples, and to all who assist you in understanding and putting into practice the Church's teaching on marriage and on responsible motherhood and fatherhood. I am thinking in particular about pastors and the many scholars, theologians, philosophers, writers and journalists who have resisted the powerful trend to cultural conformity and are courageously ready to "swim against the tide". This encouragement also goes to an increasing number of experts, physicians and educators who are authentic lay apostles for whom the promotion of the dignity of marriage and the family has become an important task in their lives. In the name of the Church I express my gratitude to all! What would priests, Bishops and even the Successor of Peter be able to do without you? From the first years of my priesthood I have become increasingly convinced of this, from when I began to sit in the *confessional* to share the concerns, fears and hopes of many married couples. I met difficult cases of rebellion and refusal, but at the same time so many marvellously responsible and generous persons! In writing this Letter I have all those married couples in mind, and I embrace them with my affection and my prayer.

*The two civilizations*

13. Dear families, the question of responsible fatherhood and motherhood is an integral part of the "civilization of love", which I now wish to discuss with you. From what has already been said it is clear that *the family is fundamental to what Pope Paul VI called the "civilization of love"*, an expression which has entered the teaching of the Church and by now has become familiar. Today it is difficult to imagine a statement by the Church, or about the Church, which does not mention the civilization of love. The phrase *is linked to the tradition of the "domestic church" in early Christianity*, but it has a particular significance for the present time. Etymologically the word "civilization" is derived from "*civis*" — "citizen", and it emphasizes the civic or political dimension of the life of every individual. But the most profound meaning of the term "civilization" is not merely political, but rather pertains to human culture. Civilization belongs to human history because it answers man's spiritual and moral needs. Created in the image and likeness of God, man has received the world from the hands of the Creator, together with the task of shaping it in his own image and likeness. The fulfilment of this task gives rise to civilization, which

in the final analysis is nothing else than the "humanization of the world".

In a certain sense civilization means the same thing as "culture". And so one could also speak of the "*culture of love*", even though it is preferable to keep to the now familiar expression. The civilization of love, in its current meaning, is inspired by the words of the conciliar Constitution *Gaudium et Spes*: "*Christ . . . fully discloses man to himself and unfolds his noble calling*". And so we can say that the civilization of love originates in the revelation of the God who "is love", as John writes (*1 Jn* 4:8, 16); it is effectively described by Paul in the hymn of charity found in his First Letter to the Corinthians (13:1-13). This civilization is intimately linked to the love "poured into our hearts through the Holy Spirit which has been given to us" (*Rom* 5:5), and it grows as a result of the *constant cultivation* which the Gospel allegory of the vine and the branches describes in such a direct way: "I am the true vine, and my Father is the vinedresser. Every branch of mine that bears no fruit, he takes away, and every branch that does bear fruit he prunes, that it may bear more fruit" (*Jn* 15:1-2).

In the light of these and other texts of the New Testament it is possible to understand what is meant by the "civilization of love", and why the *family is organically linked to this civilization*. If the first "way of the Church" is the family, it should also be said that the civilization of love is also the "way of the Church", which journeys through the world and summons families to this way; it summons also other social, national and international institutions, because of families and through families. *The family in fact depends* for several reasons *on the civilization of love*, and finds therein the reasons for its existence as family. And at the same time *the family is the centre and the heart of the civilization of love.*

Yet there is no true love without an awareness that God "is Love"—and that man is the only creature on earth which God has called into existence "for its own sake". Created in the image and likeness of God, man cannot fully "find himself" except through the sincere gift of self. Without such a concept of man, of the person and the "communion of persons" in the family, there can be no civilization of love; similarly, without the civilization of love it is impossible to have *such a concept of person and of the communion of persons*. The family constitutes the fundamental "cell" of society. But Christ—the "vine" from which the "branches" draw nourishment—is needed so that this cell will not be exposed to the threat of a kind of *cultural uprooting* which can come both from within and from without. Indeed, although there is on the one hand the "civilization of love", there continues to exist on the other hand *the possibility of a destructive "anti-civilization"*, as so many present trends and situations confirm.

Who can deny that our age is one marked by a great crisis, which appears above all as a profound "*crisis of truth*"? A crisis of truth means, in the first place, a *crisis of concepts*. Do the words "love", "freedom", "sincere gift", and even "person" and "rights of the person", really convey their essential meaning? This is why the Encyclical on the "splendour of truth" (*Veritatis Splendor*) has proved so meaningful and important for the Church and for the world—especially in the West. Only if the truth about freedom and the communion of persons in marriage and in the family can regain its splendour, will the building of the civilization of love truly begin and will it then be possible to speak concretely—as the Council did—about "promoting the dignity of marriage and the family".

Why is the "splendour of truth" so important? First of all, by way of contrast: the development of contemporary civilization is linked to a scientific and technological progress which is often achieved in a one-sided way, and thus appears purely positivistic. Positivism, as we know, results in agnosticism in theory and utilitarianism in practice and in ethics. In our own day, history is in a way repeating itself. *Utilitarianism* is a civilization of production and of use, a civilization of "things" and not of "persons", a civilization in which persons are used in the same way as things are used. In the context of a civilization of use, woman can become an object for man, children a hindrance to parents, the family an institution obstructing the freedom of its members. To be convinced that this is the case, one need only look at *certain sexual education programmes* introduced into the schools, often notwithstanding the disagreement and even the protests of many parents; or *pro-abortion tendencies* which vainly try to hide behind the so-called "right to choose" ("*pro-choice*") on the part of both spouses, and in particular on the part of the woman. These are only two examples; many more could be mentioned.

It is evident that in this sort of a cultural situation the family cannot fail to feel threatened, since it is endangered at its very foundations. Everything *contrary to the civilization of love* is contrary to the whole truth about man and becomes a threat to him: it does not allow him to find himself and to feel secure, as spouse, parent, or child. So-called "safe sex", which is touted by the "civilization of technology", is actually, in view of the overall requirements of the person, radically *not safe*, indeed it is extremely dangerous. It endangers both the person and the family. And what is this danger? It is *the loss of the truth about one's own self and about the family*, together with the risk of a loss of *freedom* and consequently of a loss of *love* itself. "You will know the truth", Jesus says, "and the truth will make you free" (*Jn* 8:32): the truth, and only the truth, will prepare you for a love which can be called "fairest love" (cf. *Sir* 24:24, Vulg.).

The contemporary family, like families in every age, *is searching for "fairest love"*. A love which is not "fairest", but reduced only to the satisfaction of concupiscence (cf. *1 Jn* 2:16), or to a man's and a woman's mutual "use" of each other, makes persons *slaves to their weaknesses*. Do not certain modern "cultural agendas" lead to this enslavement? There are agendas which "play" on man's weaknesses, and thus make him increasingly weak and defenceless.

*The civilization of love evokes joy*: joy, among other things, for the fact that a man has come into the world (cf. *Jn* 16:21), and consequently because spouses have become parents. The civilization of love means "rejoicing in the right" (cf. *1 Cor* 13:6). But a civilization inspired by a consumerist, anti-birth mentality is not and cannot ever be a civilization of love. If the family is so important for the civilization of love, it is because of the particular *closeness and intensity of the bonds* which come to be between persons and generations within the family. However, the family remains *vulnerable* and can easily fall prey to dangers which weaken it or actually destroy its unity and stability. As a result of these dangers families cease to be witnesses of the civilization of love and can even become a negation of it, a kind of *counter-sign*. A broken family can, for its part, consolidate a specific form of "anti-civilization", destroying love in its various expressions, with inevitable consequences for the whole of life in society.

*Love is demanding*

14. The love which the Apostle Paul celebrates in the First Letter to the Corinthians—the love which is

*"patient"* and *"kind"*, and *"endures all things"* (*1 Cor* 13:4, 7) — is certainly *a demanding love*. But this is precisely the source of its beauty: by the very fact that it is demanding, it builds up the true good of man and allows it to radiate to others. The good, says Saint Thomas, is by its nature "diffusive". Love is true when *it creates the good of persons and of communities*; it creates that good and *gives it* to others. Only the one who is able to be demanding with himself in the name of love can also demand love from others. Love is demanding. It makes demands in all human situations; it is even more demanding in the case of those who are open to the Gospel. Is this not what Christ proclaims in "his" commandment? Nowadays people need to rediscover this demanding love, for it is the truly firm foundation of the family, a foundation able to "endure all things". According to the Apostle, love is not able to "endure all things" if it yields to "jealousies", or if it is "boastful … arrogant or rude" (cf. *1 Cor* 13:5-6). True love, Saint Paul teaches, is different: "Love believes all things, hopes all things, endures all things" (*1 Cor* 13:7). This is the very love which "endures all things". At work within it is the power and strength of God himself, who "is love" (*1 Jn* 4:8, 16). At work within it is also the

power and strength of Christ, the Redeemer of man and Saviour of the world.

Meditating on the thirteenth chapter of the First Letter of Paul to the Corinthians, we set out on a path which leads us to understand quickly and clearly the full truth about the civilization of love. No other biblical text expresses this truth so simply and so profoundly as the *hymn to love*.

The dangers faced by love are also dangers for the civilization of love, because they promote everything capable of effectively opposing it. Here one thinks first of all of *selfishness*, not only the selfishness of individuals, but also of couples or, even more broadly, of social selfishness, that for example of a class or nation (nationalism). Selfishness in all its forms is directly and radically opposed to the civilization of love. But is love to be defined simply as "anti-selfishness"? This would be a very impoverished and ultimately a purely negative definition, even though it is true that different forms of selfishness must be overcome in order to realize love and the civilization of love. It would be more correct to speak of "altruism", which is the opposite of selfishness. But far richer and more complete is the concept of love illustrated by Saint Paul.

# The Civilization of Love

The hymn to love in the First Letter to the Corinthians remains the *Magna Charta* of the civilization of love. In this concept, what is important is not so much individual actions (whether selfish or altruistic), so much as the radical acceptance of the understanding of man as a person who "finds himself" by making a sincere gift of self. A gift is, obviously, "for others": this is *the most important dimension* of the civilization of love.

We thus come to the very heart of the Gospel truth about *freedom*. The person realizes himself by the exercise of freedom in truth. Freedom cannot be understood as a license to do *absolutely anything*: it means a *gift of self*. Even more: it means an *interior discipline of the gift*. The idea of gift contains not only the free initiative of the subject, but also the aspect of *duty*. All this is made real in the "communion of persons". We find ourselves again at the very heart of each family.

Continuing this line of thought, we also *come upon the antithesis between individualism and personalism*. Love, the civilization of love, is bound up with personalism. Why with personalism? And *why does individualism threaten the civilization of love*? We find a key to answering this in the Council's expression, a "sincere gift". Individualism presupposes a use of freedom in which the subject does what he wants, in which he himself is the one to "establish the truth" of whatever he finds pleasing or useful. He does not tolerate the fact that someone else "wants" or demands something from him in the name of an objective truth. He does not want to "give" to another on the basis of truth; he does not want to become a "sincere gift". Individualism thus remains egocentric and selfish. The real antithesis between individualism and personalism emerges not only on the level of theory, but even more *on that of "ethos"*. The "ethos" of personalism is altruistic: it moves the person to become a gift for others and to discover joy in giving himself. This is the joy about which Christ speaks (cf. *Jn* 15:11; 16:20, 22).

What is needed then is for human societies, and the families who live within them, often in a context of struggle between the civilization of love and its opposites, to seek their solid foundation in a correct vision of man and of everything which determines the full "realization" of his humanity. *Opposed to the civilization of love* is certainly the phenomenon of so-called *"free love"*; this is particularly dangerous because it is usually suggested as a way of following one's "real" feelings, but it is in fact destructive of love. How many families have been ruined because of "free love"! To follow in every instance a "real" emotional impulse by invoking a love "liberated" from all conditionings, means nothing more than to make the individual a slave to those human instincts which Saint Thomas calls "passions of the soul". "Free love" exploits human weaknesses; it gives them a certain "veneer" of respectability with the help of seduction and the blessing of public opinion. In this way there is an attempt to "soothe" consciences by creating a "moral alibi". But not all of the consequences are taken into consideration, especially when the ones who end up paying are, apart from the other spouse, the children, deprived of a father or mother and condemned to be in fact *orphans of living parents*.

As we know, at the foundation of ethical utilitarianism there is the continual quest for "maximum" happiness. But this is a "*utilitarian happiness*", seen only as pleasure, as immediate gratification for the exclusive benefit of the individual, apart from or opposed to the objective demands of the true good.

The programme of utilitarianism, based on an individualistic understanding of freedom—*a freedom without responsibilities* — is the opposite of love, even as an expression of human civilization considered as a whole. When this concept of freedom is embraced by society, and quickly allies itself with varied forms of human weakness, it soon proves a systematic and permanent threat to the family. In this regard, one could mention many dire consequences, which can be statistically verified, even though a great number of them are hidden in the hearts of men and women like painful, fresh wounds.

*The love of spouses and parents has the capacity to cure these kinds of wounds,* provided the dangers alluded to do not deprive it of its regenerative force, which is so beneficial and wholesome a thing for human communities. This capacity depends on the divine grace of forgiveness and reconciliation, which always ensures the spiritual energy to begin anew. For this very reason family members need to encounter Christ in the Church through the wonderful Sacrament of Penance and Reconciliation.

In this context, we can realize how important *prayer* is with families and for families, in particular for those threatened by division. We need to pray that married couples *will love their vocation,* even when the road becomes difficult, or the paths become narrow, uphill and seemingly insuperable; we need to pray that, even then, they will be faithful to their covenant with God.

"The family is the way of the Church". In this Letter we wish both to profess and to proclaim *this way*, which leads to the kingdom of heaven (cf. Mt 7:14) through conjugal and family life. It is important that the "communion of persons" in the family should become a preparation for the "communion of Saints". This is why the Church both believes and proclaims the love which "endures all things" (*1 Cor* 13:7); with Saint Paul she sees in it "*the greatest*" virtue of all (cf. *1 Cor* 13:13). The Apostle puts no limits on anyone. Everyone is called to love, including spouses and families. In the Church everyone is called equally to perfect holiness (cf. Mt 5:48).

*The fourth commandment:*
*"Honour your father and your mother"*

15. The fourth commandment of the Decalogue deals with the family and its interior unity—its solidarity, we could say.

In its formulation, the fourth commandment does not explicitly mention the family. In fact, however, this is its real subject matter. In order to bring out the communion between generations, *the divine Legislator could find no more appropriate word than this*: "Honour ..." (*Ex* 20:12). Here we meet another way of expressing what the family is. This formulation does not exalt the family in some "artificial" way, but emphasizes its subjectivity and the rights flowing from it. The family is a community of particularly intense interpersonal relationships: between spouses, between parents and children, between generations. It is a community which must be safeguarded in a special way. And God cannot find a better safeguard than this: "Honour".

"Honour your father and your mother, that your days may be long in the land which the Lord your God gives to you" (*Ex* 20:12). This commandment comes after the three basic precepts which concern the relation of the individual and the people of Israel with God: "*Shema, Izrael ...*", "Hear, O Israel: the Lord our God is one Lord" (*Dt* 6:4). "You will have no other gods before me" (*Ex* 20:3). This is the first and greatest commandment, the commandment of love for God "above all else": God is to be loved "with all your heart, and with all your soul, and with all your might" (*Dt* 6:5; cf. *Mt* 22:37). It is significant that the fourth commandment is placed in

64

this particular context. "Honour your father and your mother", because for you they are in a certain sense representatives of the Lord; they are the ones who gave you life, who introduced you to human existence in a particular family line, nation and culture. After God, they are your first benefactors. While God alone is good, indeed the Good itself, parents participate in this supreme goodness in a unique way. And so, honour your parents! *There is a certain analogy* here *with the worship owed to God.*

*The fourth commandment* is closely linked to the *commandment of love.* The bond between "honour" and "love" is a deep one. Honour, at its very centre, is connected with the virtue of justice, but the latter, for its part, cannot be explained fully without reference to love: the love of God and of one's neighbour. And who is more of a neighbour than one's own family members, parents and children?

Is the system of interpersonal relations indicated by the fourth commandment one-sided? Does it bind us only to honour our parents? Taken literally, it does. But indirectly we can speak of the *"honour" owed to children by their parents.* "To honour" means to acknowledge! We could put it this way: "let yourself be guided by the firm acknowledgment of the person, first of all that of your father and mother, and then that of the other members of the family". Honour is essentially an attitude of unselfishness. It could be said that it is "a sincere gift of person to person", and in that sense honour converges with love. If the fourth commandment demands that honour should be shown to our father and mother, it also makes this demand out of concern for the good of the family. Precisely for this reason, however, it makes demands of the parents themselves. You parents, the divine precept seems to say, should act in such a way that your life *will merit the honour* (and the love) of your children! Do not let the divine command that you be honoured fall into a moral vacuum! Ultimately then we are speaking of *mutual honour*. The commandment "honour your father and your mother" indirectly tells parents: Honour your sons and your daughters. They deserve this because they are alive, because they are who they are, and this is true from the first moment of their conception. The fourth commandment then, by expressing the intimate bonds uniting the family, highlights the basis of its inner unity.

The commandment goes on to say: "*that your days may be long in the land* which the Lord your God gives you".

The conjunction "that" might give the impression of an almost "utilitarian" calculation: honour them so that you will have a long life. In any event, this does not lessen the fundamental meaning of the imperative "*honour*", which by its nature suggests an *attitude of unselfishness*. To honour never means: "calculate the benefits". It is difficult, on the other hand, not to acknowledge the fact that an attitude of mutual honour among members of the family community also brings certain advantages. *"Honour" is certainly something useful*, just as every true good is "useful".

In the first place, the family achieves the good of "being together". This is the good par excellence of marriage (hence its indissolubility) and of the family community. It could also be defined as a good of the subject as such. Just as the person is a subject, so too is the family, since it is made up of persons, who, joined together by a profound bond of communion, form a single *communal subject*. Indeed, the family is more a subject than any other social institution: more so than the nation or the State, more so than society and international organizations. These societies, especially nations, possess a proper subjectivity to the extent that they receive it from persons and their families. Are all these merely "theoretical" observations, formulated for the purpose of "exalting" the family before public opinion? No, but they are another way of expressing what the family is. And this too can be deduced from the fourth commandment.

This truth deserves to be emphasized and more deeply understood: indeed it brings out the importance of the fourth commandment for the modern system of *human rights*. Institutions and legal systems employ juridical language. But God says: "honour". All "human rights" are ultimately fragile and ineffective, if at their root they lack the command to "honour"; in other words, if they lack *an acknowledgment of the individual* simply because he is an individual, "this" individual. *Of themselves, rights are not enough.*

It is not an exaggeration to reaffirm that the life of nations, of states, and of international organizations "passes" through the family and "is based" on the fourth commandment of the Decalogue. The age in which we live, notwithstanding the many juridical Declarations which have been drafted, *is still threatened to a great extent by "alienation"*. This is the result of "Enlightenment" premises according to which a man is "more" human if he is "only" human. It is not difficult to notice how alienation from everything belonging in various ways to the full richness of man threatens our times. And this affects the family. Indeed, *the affirmation of the person* is in great measure to be referred back *to the family* and consequently to the fourth commandment. In God's plan the family is in many ways the first school of how to be human. *Be human!* This is the imperative passed on in the family — human as the son or daughter of one's country, a citizen of the State, and, we would say today, a citizen of the world. The God who gave humanity the fourth commandment is "benevolent" towards man (*philanthropos*, as the Greeks said). The Creator of the universe is *the God of love and of life*: he wants man to have life and have it abundantly, as Christ proclaims (cf. *Jn* 10:10); that he may have life, first of all thanks to the family.

At this point it seems clear that the "civilization of love" is strictly bound up with the family. *For many people the civilization of love is still a pure utopia.* Indeed, there are those who think that love cannot be demanded from anyone and that it cannot be imposed: love should be a free choice which people can take or leave.

There is some truth in all this. And yet there is always the fact that Jesus Christ left us the commandment of love, just as God on Mount Sinai ordered: "Honour your father and your mother". Love then is not a utopia: it is given to mankind as a task to be carried out with the help of divine grace. It is entrusted to man and woman, in the Sacrament of Matrimony, as the basic principle of their "duty", and it becomes the foundation of their mutual responsibility: first as spouses, then as father and mother. In the celebration of the Sacrament, the spouses give and receive each other, declaring their willingness to welcome children and to educate them. On this hinges human civilization, which cannot be defined as anything other than a "civilization of love".

The family is an expression and source of this love. *Through the family passes the primary current of the civilization of love*, which finds therein its "social foundations".

The Fathers of the Church, in the Christian tradition, have spoken of the family as a "domestic church", a "little church". They thus referred to the civilization of love as a possible system of human life and coexistence: "to be together" as a family, to be for one another, to make room in a community for affirming each person as such, for affirming "this" individual person. At times it is a matter of people with physical or psychological handicaps, of whom the so-called "progressive" society would prefer to be free. Even the family can end up like this kind of society. It does so when it hastily rids itself of people who are aged, disabled or sick. This happens when there is a loss of faith in that God *for whom "all live"* (cf. *Lk* 20:38) and are called to the fullness of Life.

Yes, *the civilization of love is possible; it is not a utopia.* But it is only possible by a constant and ready reference to the "Father from whom all fatherhood on earth is named" (cf. *Eph* 3:14-15), from whom every human family comes.

## Education

16. *What is involved in raising children?* In answering this question two fundamental truths should be kept in mind: first, that man is called to live in truth and love; and second, that everyone finds fulfilment through the sincere gift of self. This is true both for the educator and for the one being educated. Education is thus a unique process for which the mutual communion of persons has immense importance. *The educator* is a person who *"begets" in a spiritual sense.* From this point of view, *raising children can be considered a genuine apostolate.* It is a living means

of communication, which not only creates a profound relationship between the educator and the one being educated, but also makes them both sharers in truth and love, that final goal to which everyone is called by God the Father, Son and Holy Spirit.

Fatherhood and motherhood presume the coexistence and interaction of autonomous subjects. This is quite evident in the case of the mother when she conceives a new human being. The first months of the child's presence in the mother's womb bring about a particular bond which already possesses an educational significance of its own. The *mother*, even before giving birth, *does not only give shape to the child's body, but also, in an indirect way, to the child's whole personality*. Even though we are speaking about a process in which the mother primarily affects the child, we should not overlook the unique influence that the unborn child has on its mother. In this *mutual influence* which will be revealed to the outside world following the birth of the child, the father does not have a direct part to play. But he should be responsibly committed to providing attention and support throughout the pregnancy and, if possible, at the moment of birth.

For the "civilization of love" it is essential that *the husband should recognize that the motherhood of his wife is a gift*: this is enormously important for the entire process of raising children. Much will depend on his willingness to take his own part in this first stage of the gift of humanity, and to become willingly involved as a husband and father in the motherhood of his wife.

Education then is before all else *a reciprocal "offering" on the part of both parents*: together they communicate their own mature humanity to the newborn child, who gives them in turn the newness and freshness of the humanity which it has brought into the world. This is the case even when children are born with mental or physical disabilities. Here, the situation of the children can enhance the very special courage needed to raise them.

With good reason, then, the Church asks during the Rite of Marriage: "Will you accept children lovingly from God, and bring them up according to the law of Christ and his Church"? In the raising of children conjugal love is expressed as authentic parental love. The "communion of persons", expressed as conjugal love at the beginning of the family, is thus completed and brought to fulfilment in the raising of children. Every individual born and raised in a family constitutes a potential treasure which must be responsibly accepted, so that it will not be diminished or lost, but will rather come to an ever more mature humanity. This too is a *process of exchange* in which the parents-educators are in turn to a certain degree educated themselves. While they are teachers of humanity for their own children, they learn humanity from them. All this clearly brings out the *organic structure of the family*, and reveals the fundamental meaning of the fourth commandment.

In rearing children, the *"we" of the parents*, of husband and wife, develops into the *"we" of the family*, which is grafted on to earlier generations, and is open to gradual expansion. In this regard both grandparents and grand-children play their own individual roles.

If it is true that by giving life *parents* share in God's creative work, it is also true that by raising their children they *become sharers in his paternal and at the same time maternal way of teaching*. According to Saint Paul, God's fatherhood is the primordial model of all fatherhood and motherhood in the universe (cf. *Eph* 3:14-15), and of hu-man motherhood and fatherhood in particular. We have been completely instructed in God's own way of teaching by the eternal Word of the Father who, by becoming man, revealed to man the authentic and integral greatness of his humanity, that is, being a child of God. In this way he also revealed the true meaning of human education. *Through Christ* all education, within the family and outside of it, *becomes part of God's own saving pedagogy*, which is addressed to individuals and families and culminates in the Paschal Mystery of the Lord's Death and Resurrection. The "heart" of our redemption is the starting-point of every process of Christian education, which is likewise always an education to a full humanity.

*Parents* are *the first and most important educators* of their own children, and they also possess a *fundamental competence* in this area: they are *educators because they are parents*. They share their educational mission with other individuals or institutions, such as the Church and the State. But the mission of education must always be carried out in accordance with a proper application of the *principle of subsidiarity*. This implies the legitimacy and indeed the need of giving assistance to the parents, but finds its intrinsic and absolute limit in their prevailing right and their actual capabilities. The principle of subsidiarity is thus at the service of parental love, meeting the good of the family unit. For parents by themselves are not capable of satisfying every requirement of the whole process of raising children, especially in matters concerning their schooling and the entire gamut of socialization. Subsidiarity thus complements paternal and maternal love and confirms its fundamental nature, inasmuch as all other participants in the process of education are only able to carry out their responsibilities *in the name of the parents, with their consent* and, to a certain degree, *with their authorization.*

The process of education ultimately leads to the phase of *self-education*, which occurs when the individual, after attaining an appropriate level of psycho-physical maturity, *begins to "educate himself on his own".* In time, self-education goes beyond the earlier results achieved by the educational process, in which it continues to be rooted. An adolescent is exposed to new people and new surroundings, particularly teachers and classmates, who exercise an influence over his life which can be either helpful or harmful. At this stage he distances himself somewhat from the education received in the family, assuming at times a critical attitude with regard to his parents. Even so, the process of self-education cannot fail to be marked by the educational influence which the family and school have on children and adolescents. Even when they grow up and set out on their own path, young people remain intimately linked to their *existential roots*.

Against this background, we can see the meaning of the fourth commandment, "*Honour your father and your mother*" (*Ex* 20:12) in a new way. It is closely linked to the whole process of education. Fatherhood and motherhood, this first and basic fact in the *gift of humanity*, open up before both parents and children new and profound perspectives. To give birth according to the flesh means to set in motion a further "birth", one which is gradual and complex and which continues in the whole process of education. The commandment of the Decalogue calls for a child to honour its father and mother. But, as we saw above, that same commandment enjoins upon parents a kind of corresponding or "symmetrical" duty. Parents are also called to "honour" their children, whether they are young or old. This attitude is needed throughout the process of their education, including the time of their schooling. The "*principle of giving honour*", the recognition and respect due to man precisely because he is a man, is the basic condition for every authentic educational process.

In the sphere of education *the Church* has a specific role to play. In the light of Tradition and the teaching of the Council, it can be said that it is not only a matter of *entrusting the Church* with the person's religious and moral education, but of promoting the entire process of the person's education *"together with"* the Church. The family is called to carry out its task of education *in the Church*, thus sharing in her life and mission. The Church wishes to carry out her educational mission above all *through families* who are made capable of undertaking this task by the Sacrament of Matrimony, through the "grace of state" which follows from it and the specific "charism" proper to the entire family community.

Certainly one area in which the family has an irreplaceable role is that of *religious education,* which enables the family to grow as a "domestic church". Religious education and the catechesis of children make the family a true *subject of evangelization and the apostolate* within the Church. We are speaking of a right intrinsically linked to the *principle of religious liberty*. Families, and more specifically parents, are free to choose for their children a particular kind of religious and moral education consonant with their own convictions. Even when they entrust these responsibilities to ecclesiastical institutions or to schools administered by religious personnel, their educational presence ought to continue to be *constant and active.*

Within the context of education, due attention must be paid to the essential question of *choosing a vocation,* and here in particular that of *preparing for marriage.* The Church has made notable efforts to promote marriage preparation, for example by offering courses for engaged couples. All this is worthwhile and necessary. But it must not be forgotten that preparing for future life as a couple is *above all the task of the family.* To be sure, only spiritually mature families can adequately assume that responsibility. Hence we should point out the need for a special *solidarity among families.* This can be expressed in various practical ways, as for example by associations of families for families. The institution of the family is strengthened by such expressions of solidarity, which bring together not only individuals but also communities, with a commitment to pray together and to seek together the answers to life's essential questions. Is this not an invaluable expression of the *apostolate of families* to one another? It is important that families attempt to build bonds of solidarity among themselves. This allows them to assist each other in the educational enterprise: parents are educated by other parents, and children by other children. Thus a particular tradition of education is created, which draws strength from the character of the "domestic church" proper to the family.

The *gospel of love* is the inexhaustible source of all that nourishes the human family as a "communion of persons". In love the whole educational process finds its support and definitive meaning as the mature fruit of the parents' mutual gift. Through the efforts, sufferings and disappointments which are part of every person's education, love is constantly being put to the test. To pass the test, a source of spiritual strength is necessary. This is only found in the One who "loved to the end" (*Jn* 13:1). Thus *education is fully a part of the "civilization of love"*. It depends on the civilization of love and, in great measure, contributes to its upbuilding.

The Church's constant and trusting prayer during the Year of the Family is *for the education of man*, so that families will persevere in their task of education with courage, trust and hope, in spite of difficulties occasionally so serious as to appear insuperable. The Church prays that the forces of the "civilization of love", which have their source in the love of God, will be triumphant. These are forces which the Church ceaselessly expends for the good of the whole human family.

*Family and society*

17. The family is a community of persons and the smallest social unit. As such it is an *institution* fundamental to the life of every society.

What does the family as an institution expect from society? First of all, it expects *a recognition of its identity* and an acceptance of its *status as a subject in society*. This "social subjectivity" is bound up with the proper identity of marriage and the family. Marriage, which undergirds the institution of the family, is constituted by the covenant whereby "a man and a woman establish between themselves a partnership of their whole life", and which "of its own very nature is ordered to the well-being of the spouses and to the procreation and upbringing of children". Only such a union can be recognized and ratified as a "marriage" in society. Other interpersonal unions which do not fulfil the above conditions cannot be recognized, despite certain growing trends which represent a serious threat to the future of the family and of society itself.

No human society can run the risk of permissiveness in fundamental issues regarding the nature of marriage and the family! Such moral permissiveness cannot fail to damage the authentic requirements of peace and communion among people. It is thus quite understandable why the Church vigorously defends the identity of the family and encourages responsible individuals and institutions, especially political leaders and international organizations, not to yield to the temptation of a superficial and false modernity.

As a community of love and life, the family is a firmly grounded social reality. It is also, in a way entirely its own, a *sovereign society*, albeit conditioned in certain ways. This affirmation of the family's sovereignty as an institution and the recognition of the various ways in which it is conditioned naturally leads to the subject of *family rights*. In this regard, the Holy See published in 1983 the *Charter of the Rights of the Family*; even today this document has lost none of its relevance.

The rights of the family are closely *linked to the rights of the person*: if in fact the family is a communion of persons, its self-realization will depend in large part on the correct application of the rights of its members. Some of these rights concern the family in an immediate way, such as the right of parents to responsible procreation and the education of children. Other rights however touch the family unit only indirectly: among these, the right to property, especially to what is called family property, and the right to work are of special importance.

But the rights of the family *are not simply the sum total* of the rights of the person, since the family is *much more* than the sum of its individual members. It is a community of parents and children, and at times a community of several generations. For this reason its "status as a subject", which is grounded in God's plan, gives rise to and calls for certain proper and specific rights. *The Charter of the Rights of the Family*, on the basis of the moral principles mentioned above, consolidates the existence of the institution of the family in the social and juridical order of the "greater" society — those of the nation, of the State and of international communities. Each of these "greater" societies is at least indirectly conditioned by the existence of the family. As a result, the definition of the rights and duties of the "greater" society

with regard to the family is an extremely important and
even essential issue.

In the first place there is the almost organic link existing between *the family and the nation*. Naturally we cannot speak in all cases about a nation in the proper sense.
Ethnic groups still exist which, without being able to
be considered true nations, do fulfil to some extent the
function of a "greater" society. In both cases, the link of
the family with the ethnic group or the nation is founded
above all on *a participation in its culture*. In one sense,
parents also give birth to children for the nation, so that
they can be members of it and can share in its historic
and cultural heritage. From the very outset the identity
of the family is to some extent shaped by the identity of
the nation to which it belongs.

By sharing in the nation's cultural heritage, the family
contributes to that *specific sovereignty*, which has its origin
in a distinct culture and language. I addressed this subject
at the UNESCO Conference meeting in Paris in 1980,
and, given its unquestionable importance, I have often
returned to it. Not only the nations, but every family realizes its *spiritual sovereignty* through culture and language.
Were this not true, it would be very difficult to explain

many events in the history of peoples, especially in Europe. From these events, ancient and modern, inspiring and painful, glorious and humiliating, it becomes clear how much the family is an organic part of the nation, and the nation of the family.

In regard to the *State*, the link with the family is somewhat similar and at the same time somewhat dissimilar. The State, in fact, is distinct from the nation; it has a less "family-like" structure, since it is organized in accordance with a political system and in a more "bureaucratic" fashion. Nonetheless, the apparatus of the State also has, in some sense, a "soul" of its own, to the extent that it lives up to its nature as a "political community" juridically ordered towards the common good. Closely linked to this "soul" is the family, which is connected with the State precisely by reason of the *principle of subsidiarity*. Indeed, the family is a social reality which does not have readily available all the means necessary to carry out its proper ends, also in matters regarding schooling and the rearing of children. The State is thus called upon to play a role in accordance with the principle mentioned above. Whenever the family is self-sufficient, it should be left to act on its own; an excessive intrusiveness on the part of the State would prove detrimental, to say nothing of lacking due respect, and would constitute an open violation of the rights of the family. Only in those situations where the family is not really self-sufficient does the State have the authority and duty to intervene.

Beyond child-rearing and schooling at all levels, State assistance, while not excluding private initiatives, can find expression in institutions such as those founded to safeguard the life and health of citizens, and in particular to provide social benefits for workers. *Unemployment* is today one of the most serious threats to family life and a rightful cause of concern to every society. It represents a challenge for the political life of individual States and an area for careful study in the Church's social doctrine. It is urgently necessary, therefore, to come up with courageous solutions capable of looking beyond the confines of one's own nation and taking into consideration the many families for whom lack of employment means living in situations of tragic poverty.

While speaking about employment in reference to the family, it is appropriate to emphasize how important and burdensome is *the work women do within the family unit: that work should be acknowledged and deeply appreciated.*

The "toil" of a woman who, having given birth to a child, nourishes and cares for that child and devotes herself to its upbringing, particularly in the early years, is so great as to be comparable to any professional work. This ought to be clearly stated and upheld, no less than any other labour right. Motherhood, because of all the hard work it entails, should be recognized as giving the right to financial benefits at least equal to those of other kinds of work undertaken in order to support the family during such a delicate phase of its life.

Every effort should be made so that the family will be recognized as the *primordial* and, in a certain sense "sovereign" *society*! The "sovereignty" of the family is essential for the good of society. A truly sovereign and spiritually vigorous nation is always made up of strong families who are aware of their vocation and mission in history. *The family is at the heart* of all these problems and tasks. To relegate it to a subordinate or secondary role, excluding it from its rightful position in society, would be to inflict grave harm on the authentic growth of society as a whole.

# The Bridegroom Is with You

*At Cana in Galilee*

18. Engaged in conversation with John's disciples one day, Jesus speaks of a wedding invitation and the presence of the bridegroom among the guests: "the Bridegroom is with them" (Mt 9:15). In this way he indicated the fulfilment in his own person of the image of God the Bridegroom, which had already been used in the Old Testament, in order to reveal fully the mystery of God as the mystery of Love.

By describing himself as a "Bridegroom", Jesus reveals the essence of God and confirms his immense love for mankind. But the choice of this image also throws light indirectly on the profound truth of spousal love. Indeed by using this image in order to speak about God, Jesus shows to what extent the fatherhood and the love of God are reflected in the love of a man and a woman united in marriage. Hence, at the beginning of his mission, we find Jesus at *Cana in Galilee*, taking part in a wedding banquet, together with Mary and with the first disciples (cf. *Jn* 2:1-11). He thus wishes to make clear *to what extent the truth about the family is part of God's Revelation and the history of salvation.* In the Old Testament, and particularly in the Prophets, we find many beautiful expressions about the *love of God.* It is a gentle love like that of a mother for her child, a tender love like that of the bridegroom for his bride, but at the same time an equally and intensely jealous love. It is not in the first place a love which chastises but one which forgives; a love which deigns to meet man just as the father does in the case of the prodigal son; a love which raises him up and gives him a share in divine life. It is an amazing love: something entirely new and previously unknown to the whole pagan world.

At Cana in Galilee Jesus is, as it were, the *herald of the divine truth about marriage,* that truth on which the human family can rely, gaining reassurance amid all the trials of life. Jesus proclaims this truth by his presence at the wedding in Cana and by working his first "sign": water changed into wine.

Jesus proclaims the truth about marriage again when, speaking to the Pharisees, he explains how the love which comes from God, a tender and spousal love, *gives rise to profound and radical demands*. Moses, by allowing a certificate of divorce to be drawn up, had been less demanding. When in their lively argument the Pharisees appealed to Moses, Jesus' answer was categorical: "from the beginning it was not so" (*Mt* 19:8). And he reminds them that the One who created man created him male and female, and ordained that "a man leaves his father and his mother and cleaves to his wife, and they become one flesh" (*Gen* 2:24). With logical consistency Jesus concludes: "So they are no longer two but one flesh. What therefore God has joined together, let not man put asunder" (*Mt* 19:6). To the objection of the Pharisees who vaunt the Law of Moses he replies: "For your hardness of heart Moses allowed you to divorce your wives, but from the beginning it was not so" (*Mt* 19:8).

Jesus appeals to "the beginning", seeing at the very origins of creation God's plan, on which the family is based, and, through the family, the entire history of humanity. What marriage is in nature becomes, by the will of Christ, a true sacrament of the New Covenant, sealed by the blood of Christ the Redeemer. *Spouses and families, remember at what price you have been "bought"!* (cf. *1 Cor* 6:20).

But it is *humanly difficult* to accept and to live this marvellous truth. Should we be surprised that Moses relented before the insistent demands of his fellow Israelites, if the Apostles themselves, upon hearing the words of the Master, reply by saying: "If such is the case of a man with his wife, it is not expedient to marry" (*Mt* 19:10)! Nonetheless, in view of the good of man and woman, of the family and the whole of society, Jesus confirms the demand which God laid down from the beginning. At the same time, however, he takes the opportunity to affirm the value of a decision not to marry for the sake of the Kingdom of God. This choice too enables one to "beget", albeit in a different way. In this choice we find the origin of the consecrated life, of the Religious Orders and Religious Congregations of East and West, and also of the discipline of priestly celibacy, as found in the tradition of the Latin Church. Hence it is untrue that "it is not expedient to marry"; however, love for the kingdom of heaven can lead a person to choose not to marry (cf. *Mt* 19:12).

# The Bridegroom Is with You

Marriage however remains *the usual human vocation*, which is embraced by the great majority of the people of God. It is in the family where living stones are formed for that spiritual house spoken of by the Apostle Peter (cf. *1 Pet* 2:5). The bodies of the husband and wife are the dwelling-place of the Holy Spirit (cf. *1 Cor* 6:19). Because the transmission of divine life presumes the transmission of human life, marriage not only brings about the birth of human children, but also, through the power of Baptism, the birth of adopted children of God, who live the new life received from Christ through his Spirit.

Dear brothers and sisters, spouses and parents, this is how the *Bridegroom is with you*. You know that he is the Good Shepherd. You know who he is, and you know his voice. You know where he is leading you, and how he strives to give you pastures where you can find life and find it in abundance. You know how he withstands the marauding wolves, and is ever ready to rescue his sheep: every husband and wife, every son and daughter, every member of your families. You know that he, as the Good Shepherd, is prepared to lay down his own life for his flock (cf. *Jn* 10:11). He leads you by paths which are not the steep and treacherous paths of many of today's ideologies, and he repeats to today's world the fullness of truth, even as he did in his conversation with the Pharisees or when he announced it to the Apostles, who then proclaimed it to all the ends of the earth and to all the people of their day, to Jews and Greeks alike. The disciples were fully conscious that Christ had made all things new. They knew that man had been made a "new creation": no longer Jew or Greek, no longer slave or free, no longer male or female, but "one" in Christ (cf. *Gal* 3:28) and endowed with the dignity of an adopted child of God. On the day of Pentecost man received the Spirit, the Comforter, the Spirit of truth. This was the beginning of the new People of God, the Church, the foreshadowing of new heavens and a new earth (cf. *Rev* 21:1).

The Apostles, overcoming their initial fears even about marriage and the family, grew in courage. They came to understand that marriage and family are a true vocation which comes from God himself and is an apostolate: the apostolate of the laity. Families are meant to contribute to the transformation of the earth and the renewal of the world, of creation and of all humanity.

Dear families, you too should be fearless, ever ready to give witness to the hope that is in you (cf. *1 Pet* 3:15), since the Good Shepherd has put that hope in your hearts through the Gospel. You should be ready to follow Christ towards the pastures of life, which he himself has prepared through the Paschal Mystery of his Death and Resurrection.

*Do not be afraid* of the risks! God's strength is always far more powerful than your difficulties! Immeasurably greater than the evil at work in the world is the power of the *Sacrament of Reconciliation*, which the Fathers of the Church rightly called a "second Baptism". Much more influential than the corruption present in the world is the divine power of the Sacrament of *Confirmation*, which brings Baptism to its maturity. And incomparably greater than all is the power of the Eucharist.

The *Eucharist* is truly a wondrous sacrament. In it Christ has given us himself as food and drink, as a source of saving power. He has left himself to us that we might have life and have it in abundance (cf. *Jn* 10:10): the life which is in him and which he has shared with us by the gift of the Spirit in rising from the dead on the third day. The life that comes from Christ is a life for us. *It is for you, dear husbands and wives, parents and families!* Did Jesus not institute the Eucharist in a family-like setting during the Last Supper? When you meet for meals and are together in harmony, *Christ is close to you.* And he is Emmanuel, God with us, in an even greater way whenever you approach the table of the Eucharist. It can happen, as it did at Emmaus, that he is recognized only in "the breaking of the bread" (cf. *Lk* 24:35). It may well be that he is knocking at the door for a long time, waiting for it to be opened so that he can enter and eat with us (cf. *Rev* 3:20). The Last Supper and the words he spoke there contain all the power and wisdom of the sacrifice of the Cross. No other power and wisdom exist by which we can be saved and through which we can help to save others. There is no other power and no other wisdom by which you, parents, can educate both your children and yourselves. The *educational power of the Eucharist* has been proved down the generations and centuries.

Everywhere the Good Shepherd is with us. Even as he was at Cana in Galilee, *the Bridegroom in the midst of the bride and groom* as they entrusted themselves to each other for their whole life, so the Good Shepherd is also with us today as the reason for our hope, the source of strength for our hearts, the wellspring of ever new enthusiasm and the sign of the triumph of the "civilization of love". Jesus, the Good Shepherd, continues to say to us: *Do not be afraid. I am with you.* "I am with you always, to the close of the age" (*Mt* 28:20). What is the source of this strength? What is the reason for our certainty that you are with us, even though they put you to death, O Son of God, and you died like any other human being? What is the reason for this certainty? The Evangelist says: "He loved them to the end" (*Jn* 13:1). Thus do you love us, you who are the First and the Last, the Living One; you who died and are alive for evermore (cf. *Rev* 1:17-18).

*The Great Mystery*

19. Saint Paul uses a concise phrase in referring to family life: it is a "*great mystery*" (*Eph* 5:32). What he writes in the Letter to the Ephesians about that "great mystery", although deeply rooted in the Book of Genesis and in the whole Old Testament tradition, nonetheless represents a new approach which will later find expression in the Church's Magisterium.

The Church professes that Marriage, as the Sacrament of the covenant between husband and wife, is a "great mystery", because it expresses *the spousal love of Christ for his Church.* Saint Paul writes: "Husbands, love your wives, as Christ loved the Church and gave himself up for her, that he might sanctify her, having cleansed her by the washing of water with the word" (*Eph* 5:25-26). The Apostle is speaking here about Baptism, which he discusses at length in the Letter to the Romans, where he presents it as a sharing in the death of Christ leading to a sharing in his life (cf. *Rom* 6:3-4). In this Sacrament the believer *is born* as a new man, for Baptism has the power to communicate new life, the very life of God. The mystery of the God-man is in some way recapitulated in the event of Baptism. As Saint Irenaeus would later say, along with many other Fathers of the Church of both East and West: "Christ Jesus, our Lord, the Son of God, became the son of man so that man could become a son of God".

The Bridegroom then is the very same God who became man. In the Old Covenant Yahweh appears as the Bridegroom of Israel, the chosen people — a Bride-groom who is both affectionate and demanding, jealous and faithful. Israel's moments of betrayal, desertion and idolatry, described in such powerful and evocative terms by the Prophets, can never extinguish the love with which *God–the Bridegroom* "loves to the end" (cf. *Jn* 13:1).

# The Bridegroom Is with You

The confirmation and fulfilment of the spousal relationship between God and his people are realized in Christ, in the New Covenant. Christ assures us that the Bridegroom is with us (cf. Mt 9:15). He is with all of us; he is with the Church. *The Church becomes a Bride*, the Bride of Christ. This Bride, of whom the Letter to the Ephesians speaks, is present in each of the baptized and is like one who presents herself before her Bridegroom. "Christ loved the Church and gave himself up for her ..., that he might present the Church to himself in splendour, without spot or wrinkle or any such thing, that she might be holy and without blemish" (*Eph* 5:25-27). The love with which the Bridegroom "has loved" the Church "to the end" continuously renews her holiness in her saints, even though she remains a Church of sinners. Even sinners, "tax collectors and harlots", are called to holiness, as Christ himself affirms in the Gospel (cf. Mt 21:31). All are called to become a glorious Church, holy and without blemish. "Be holy", says the Lord, "for I am holy" (*Lev* 11:44; cf. *1 Pet* 1:16).

This is the deepest significance of the "great mystery", the inner meaning of the *sacramental gift* in the Church, the most profound meaning of Baptism and the Eucharist.

They are fruits of the love with which the Bridegroom has loved us to the end, a love which continually expands and lavishes on people an ever greater sharing in the supernatural life.

Saint Paul, after having said: "Husbands, love your wives" (*Eph* 5:25), emphatically adds: "Even so husbands should love their wives as their own bodies. He who loves his wife loves himself. For no man ever hates his own flesh, but nourishes and cherishes it, as Christ does the Church, because we are members of his body" (*Eph* 5:28-30). And he encourages spouses with the words: "Be subject to one another out of reverence for Christ" (*Eph* 5:21).

This is unquestionably a new presentation of the eternal truth about marriage and the family in the light of the New Covenant. Christ has revealed this truth in the Gospel by his presence at Cana in Galilee, by the sacrifice of the Cross and the Sacraments of his Church. Husbands and wives thus discover in Christ *the point of reference for their spousal love*. In speaking of Christ as the Bridegroom of the Church, Saint Paul uses the analogy of spousal love, referring back to the Book of Genesis: "A man leaves his father and his mother and cleaves to his wife, and they become one flesh" (*Gen* 2:24). This is the "great mystery" of that eternal love already present in creation, revealed in Christ and entrusted to the Church. "This mystery is a profound one", the Apostle repeats, "and I am saying that it refers to Christ and the Church" (*Eph* 5:32). The Church cannot therefore be understood as the Mystical Body of Christ, as the sign of man's Covenant with God in Christ, or as the universal sacrament of salvation, unless we keep in mind the "great mystery" involved in the creation of man as male and female and the vocation of both to conjugal love, to fatherhood and to motherhood. The "great mystery", which is the Church and humanity in Christ, does not exist apart from the "great mystery" expressed in the "one flesh" (cf. *Gen* 2:24; *Eph* 5:31-32), that is, in the reality of marriage and the family.

The family itself is the great mystery of God. As the "domestic church", it is the *bride of Christ*. The universal Church, and every particular Church in her, is most immediately revealed as the bride of Christ in the "domestic church" and in its experience of love: conjugal love, paternal and maternal love, fraternal love, the love of a community of persons and of generations. Could we even imagine human love without the Bridegroom and the love with which he first loved to the end? Only if husbands and wives share in that love and in that "great mystery" can they love "to the end". Unless they share in it, they do not know "to the end" what love truly is and how radical are its demands. And this is undoubtedly very dangerous for them.

The teaching of the Letter to the Ephesians amazes us with its depth and the *authority of its ethical teaching*. Pointing to marriage, and indirectly to the family, as the "great mystery" which refers to Christ and the Church, the Apostle Paul is able to reaffirm what he had earlier said to husbands: "Let each one of you love his wife as himself". He goes on to say: "And let the wife see that she respects her husband" (*Eph* 5:33). Respect, because she loves and knows that she is loved in return. It is because of this love that husband and wife *become a mutual gift*. Love contains the acknowledgment of the personal dignity of the other, and of his or her absolute uniqueness. Indeed, each of the spouses, as a human being, has been willed by God from among all the creatures of the earth for his or her own sake. Each of them, however, by a conscious and responsible act, makes a free gift of self to the other and to the children received from the Lord.

It is significant that Saint Paul continues his exhortation by echoing the fourth commandment: "Children, obey your parents in the Lord, for this is right. 'Honour your father and mother' (this is the first commandment with a promise), 'that it may be well with you and that you may live long on the earth'. Fathers, do not provoke your children to anger, but bring them up in the discipline and instruction of the Lord" (*Eph* 6:1-4). The Apostle thus sees in the fourth commandment the implicit commitment of mutual respect between husband and wife, between parents and children, and he recognizes in it the *principle of family stability*.

Saint Paul's magnificent synthesis concerning the "great mystery" appears as the compendium or *summa*, in some sense, *of the teaching about God and man* which was brought to fulfilment by Christ. Unfortunately, Western thought, with the development of *modern rationalism*, has been gradually moving away from this teaching. The philosopher who formulated the principle of "*Cogito, ergo sum*", "I think, therefore I am", also gave the modern concept of man its distinctive dualistic character. It is typical of rationalism to make a radical contrast in man between spirit and body, between body and spirit. But man is a person in the unity of his body and his spirit. The body can never be reduced to mere matter: it is a *spiritualized body*, just as man's spirit is so closely united to the body that he can be described as *an embodied spirit*. The richest source for knowledge of the body is the Word made flesh. *Christ reveals man to himself*. In a certain sense this statement of the Second Vatican Council is the reply, so long awaited, which the Church has given to modern rationalism.

This reply is of fundamental importance for understanding the family, especially against the background of today's civilization, which, as has been said, seems in so many cases to have given up the attempt to be a "civilization of love". The modern age has made great progress in understanding both the material world and human psychology, but with regard to his deepest, metaphysical dimension contemporary man remains to a great extent a *being unknown* to himself. Consequently the family too remains an *unknown reality*. Such is the result of estrangement from that "great mystery" spoken of by the Apostle.

The separation of spirit and body in man has led to a growing tendency to consider the human body, not in accordance with the categories of its specific likeness to

God, but rather on the basis of its similarity to all the other bodies present in the world of nature, bodies which man uses as raw material in his efforts to produce goods for consumption. But everyone can immediately realize what enormous dangers lurk behind the application of such criteria to man. When the human body, considered apart from spirit and thought, comes to be used as *raw material* in the same way that the bodies of animals are used—and this actually occurs for example in experimentation on embryos and fetuses—we will inevitably arrive at a dreadful ethical defeat.

Within a similar anthropological perspective, the human family is facing the challenge of a *new Manichaeanism*, in which body and spirit are put in radical opposition; the body does not receive life from the spirit, and the spirit does not give life to the body. Man thus *ceases to live as a person and a subject*. Regardless of all intentions and declarations to the contrary, he becomes merely an *object*. This neo-Manichaean culture has led, for example, to human sexuality being regarded more as an area *for manipulation and exploitation* than as the basis of that *primordial wonder* which led Adam on the morning of creation to exclaim before Eve: "This at last is bone of my bones and flesh of my flesh" (*Gen* 2:23). This same wonder is echoed in the words of the Song of Solomon: "You have ravished my heart, my sister, my bride, you have ravished my heart with a glance of your eyes" (*Song* 4:9). How far removed are some modern ideas from the profound understanding of masculinity and femininity found in Divine Revelation! Revelation leads us to discover in *human sexuality* a *treasure proper to the person*, who finds true fulfilment in the family but who can likewise express his profound calling in virginity and in celibacy for the sake of the Kingdom of God.

Modern rationalism *does not tolerate mystery*. It does not accept the mystery of man as male and female, nor is it willing to admit that the full truth about man has been revealed in Jesus Christ. In particular, it does not accept the "great mystery" proclaimed in the Letter to the Ephesians, but radically opposes it. It may well acknowledge, in the context of a vague deism, the possibility and even the need for a supreme or divine Being, but it firmly rejects the idea of a God who became man in order to save man. For rationalism it is unthinkable that God should be the Redeemer, much less *that he should be "the Bridegroom"*, the primordial and unique source of the human love between spouses. Rationalism provides a radically different way of looking at creation and the meaning of human existence. But once man begins to lose sight of a God who loves him, a God who calls man through Christ to live in him and with him, and once the family no longer has the possibility of sharing in the "great mystery", what is left except the mere *temporal dimension of life*? Earthly life becomes nothing more than the scenario of a battle for existence, of a desperate search for gain, and financial gain before all else.

The deep-seated roots of the "great mystery", the sacrament of love and life which began with Creation and Redemption and which *has Christ the Bridegroom as its ultimate surety*, have been lost in the modern way of looking at things. The "great mystery" is threatened in us and all around us. May the Church's celebration of the Year of the Family be a fruitful opportunity for husbands and wives to rediscover that mystery and recommit themselves to it with strength, courage and enthusiasm.

*Mother of Fairest Love*

20. The history of "fairest love" begins at the Annunciation, in those wondrous words which the angel spoke to

Mary, called to become the Mother of the Son of God. With Mary's "yes", the One who is "God from God and Light from Light" becomes a son of man. Mary is his Mother, while continuing to be the Virgin who "knows not man" (cf. *Lk* 1:34). As Mother and Virgin, *Mary* becomes the *Mother of Fairest Love*. This truth is already revealed in the words of the Archangel Gabriel, but its full significance will gradually become clearer and more evident as Mary follows her Son in the pilgrimage of faith.

The "Mother of Fairest Love" was accepted by the one who, according to Israel's tradition, was already her earthly husband: *Joseph, of the house of David.* Joseph would have had the right to consider his promised bride as his wife and the mother of his children. But God takes it upon himself to intervene in this spousal covenant: "Joseph, son of David, do not fear to take Mary as your wife, for that which is conceived in her is of the Holy Spirit" (*Mt* 1:20). Joseph is aware, having seen it with his own eyes, that a new life with which he has had nothing to do has been conceived in Mary. Being a just man, and observing the Old Law, which in his situation imposed the obligation of divorce, he wishes to dissolve his marriage in a loving way (cf. *Mt* 1:19). The angel of the Lord tells him that this would not be consistent with his vocation; indeed it would be contrary to the spousal love uniting him to Mary. This mutual spousal love, to be completely "fairest love", requires that he should take Mary and her Son into his own house in Nazareth. Joseph obeys the divine message and does all that he had been commanded (cf. *Mt* 1:24). And so, thanks also to Joseph, the *mystery of the Incarnation* and, together with it, the mystery of the Holy Family, *come to be profoundly inscribed in the spousal love of husband and wife* and, in an indirect way, in the genealogy of every human family. What Saint Paul will call the "great mystery" found its most lofty expression in the Holy Family. Thus the *family* truly takes its place *at the very heart of the New Covenant*.

It can also be said that the history of "fairest love" began, in a certain way, with the *first human couple*: Adam and Eve. The temptation to which they yielded and the original sin which resulted did not completely deprive them of the capacity for "fairest love". This becomes clear when we read, for example, in the Book of Tobit that the spouses Tobias and Sarah, in defining the meaning of their union, appealed to their first parents, Adam and Eve (cf. *Tob* 8:6). In the New Covenant, Saint Paul also bears witness to this, speaking of Christ as a new Adam (cf. *1 Cor* 15:45). Christ does not come to condemn the first Adam and the first Eve, but to save them. He comes to renew everything that is God's gift in man, everything in him that is eternally good and beautiful, everything that forms the basis of "fairest love". The *history of "fairest love"* is, in one sense, the *history of man's salvation.*

"Fairest love" always *begins with the self-revelation of the person.* At creation Eve reveals herself to Adam, just as Adam reveals himself to Eve. In the course of history newly-married couples tell each other: "We shall walk the path of life together". The family thus begins as a union of the two and, through the Sacrament, as a new community in Christ. *For love to be truly "fairest", it must be a gift of God,* grafted by the Holy Spirit on to human hearts and continually nourished in them (cf.*Rom* 5:5). Fully conscious of this, the Church in the Sacrament of Marriage asks the Holy Spirit to visit human hearts. If love is truly to be "fairest love", a gift of one person to another, it must come from the One who is himself a gift and the source of every gift.

Such was the case, as the Gospel recounts, with Mary and Joseph who, at the threshold of the New Covenant, renewed the experience of "fairest love" described in the Song of Solomon. Joseph thinks of Mary in the words: "My sister, my bride" (*Song* 4:9). Mary, the Mother of God, conceives by the power of the Holy Spirit, who is the origin of the "fairest love", which the Gospel delicately places in the context of the "great mystery".

When we speak about "fairest love", we are also speaking about *beauty:* the beauty of love and the beauty of the human being who, by the power of the Holy Spirit, is capable of such love. We are speaking of the beauty of man and woman: their beauty as brother or sister, as a couple about to be married, as husband and wife. The Gospel sheds light not only on the mystery of "fairest love", but also on the equally profound mystery of beauty, which, like love, is from God. Man and woman are from God, two persons called to become a mutual gift. From the primordial gift of the Spirit, the "giver of life", there arises the reciprocal gift of being husband or wife, no less than that of being brother or sister.

All this is confirmed by the mystery of the Incarnation, a mystery which has been *the source of a new beauty* in the history of humanity and has inspired countless masterpieces of art. After the strict prohibition against portraying the invisible God by graven images (cf. *Dt* 4:15-20), the Christian era began instead to portray in art the God who became man, Mary his Mother, Saint Joseph, the Saints of the Old and New Covenant and the entire created world redeemed by Christ. In this way it began a new relationship with the world of culture and of art. It can be said that this *new artistic canon*, attentive to the deepest dimension of man and his future, originates in the mystery of Christ's Incarnation and draws inspiration from the mysteries of his life: his birth in Bethlehem, his hidden life in Nazareth, his public ministry, Golgotha, the Resurrection and his final return in glory. The Church is conscious that her presence in the contemporary world, and in particular the contribution and support she offers to the promotion of the dignity of marriage and the family, are intimately linked to the development of culture, and she is rightly concerned for this. This is precisely why the Church is so concerned with the direction taken by the means of social communication, which have the duty of *forming* as well as *informing* their vast audience. Knowing the vast and powerful impact of the media, she never tires of reminding communications workers of the dangers arising from the manipulation of truth. Indeed, what truth can there be in films, shows and radio and television programmes dominated by pornography and violence? Do these really serve the *truth about man*? Such questions are unavoidable for those who work in the field of communications and those who have responsibility for creating and marketing media products.

This kind of critical reflection should lead our society, which certainly contains many positive aspects on the material and cultural level, to realize that, from various points of view, it is a *society which is sick* and is creating profound distortions in man. Why is this happening? The reason is that our society has broken away from the full truth about man, from the truth about what man and woman really are as persons. Thus it cannot adequately comprehend the real meaning of the gift of persons in marriage, responsible love at the service of fatherhood and motherhood, and the true grandeur of procreation and education. Is it an exaggeration to say that the *mass media*, if they are not guided by sound ethical principles, fail to serve the truth in its fundamental dimension? This is the real drama: the modern means of social communication are tempted to manipulate the message, *thereby falsifying the truth about man*. Human beings are not the same thing as the images proposed in advertising and shown by the modern mass media. *They are much more*, in their physical and psychic unity, as composites of soul and body, as persons. They are much more because of their vocation to love, which introduces them as male and female into the realm of the "great mystery".

Mary was the first to enter this realm, and she introduced her husband Joseph into it. Thus they became the *first models* of that "fairest love" which the Church continually implores for young people, husbands and wives and families. Young people, spouses and families themselves should never cease to pray for this. How can we not think about the crowds of pilgrims, old and young, who visit Marian shrines and gaze upon the face of the Mother of God, on the faces of the Holy Family, where they find reflected the full beauty of the love which God has given to mankind?

In the Sermon on the Mount, recalling the sixth commandment, Christ proclaims: "You have heard that it was said, 'You shall not commit adultery'. But I say to you that every one who looks at a woman lustfully has already committed adultery with her in his heart" (Mt 5:27-28). With regard to the Decalogue and its purpose of defending the traditional solidity of marriage and the family, these words represent a great step forward. Jesus goes to the very source of the sin of adultery, which dwells in the innermost heart of man and is revealed in a way of looking and thinking dominated by *concupiscence*. Through concupiscence *man tends to treat as his own possession another human being,* one who does not belong to him but to God. In speaking to his contemporaries, Christ is also speaking to men and women in every age and generation. He is speaking in particular to our own generation, living as it is in a society marked by consumerism and hedonism.

Why does Christ speak out in so forceful and demanding a way in the Sermon on the Mount? The reason is quite clear: Christ wants to safeguard *the holiness of marriage and of the family*. He wants to defend the full truth about the human person and his dignity.

Only in the light of this truth can the family be "to the end" the great "revelation", the *first discovery of the other*: the mutual discovery of husband and wife and then of each son and daughter born to them. All that a husband and a wife promise to each other—to be "true in good times and in bad, and to love and honour each other all the days of their life" — is possible only when "fairest love" is present. Man today cannot learn this from what modern mass culture has to say. "Fairest love" is learned above all in prayer. *Prayer*, in fact, always brings with it, to use an expression of Saint Paul, a type of *interior hiddenness with Christ in God; "your life is hid with Christ in God"* (*Col* 3:3). Only in this hiddenness do we see the workings of the Holy Spirit, the source of "fairest love". He has poured forth this love not only in the hearts of Mary and Joseph but also in the hearts of all married couples who are open to hearing the word of God and keeping it (cf. *Lk* 8:15). The future of each family unit depends upon this "fairest love": the mutual love of husband and wife, of parents and children, a love embracing all generations. Love is the true *source of the unity and strength of the family*.

*Birth and Danger*

21. It is significant that the brief account of the infancy of Jesus mentions, practically at the same time, his *birth* and the *danger* which he immediately had to confront. Luke records the prophetic words uttered by the aged Simeon when the Child was presented to the Lord in

the Temple forty days after his birth. Simeon speaks of "light" and of a "sign of contradiction". He goes on to predict of Mary: "And a sword will pierce through your own soul also" (cf. *Lk* 2:32-35). Matthew, for his part, tells of the plot of Herod against Jesus. Informed by the Magi who came from the East to see the new king who was to be born (cf. *Mt* 2:2), Herod senses a threat to his power, and after their departure he orders the death of all male children aged two years or under in Bethlehem and the surrounding towns. Jesus escapes from the hands of Herod thanks to a special divine intervention and the fatherly care of Joseph, who takes him with his mother into Egypt, where they remain until Herod's death. The Holy Family then returns to Nazareth, their home town, and begins what for many years would be a hidden life, marked by the carrying out of daily tasks with fidelity and generosity (cf. *Mt* 2:1-23; *Lk* 2:39-52).

The fact that Jesus, from his very birth, had to face threats and dangers has a certain *prophetic eloquence*. Even as a Child, Jesus is a "sign of contradiction". Prophetically eloquent also is the tragedy of the innocent children of Bethlehem, slaughtered at Herod's command. According to the Church's ancient liturgy, they shared in the birth and saving passion of Christ. Through their own "passion", they complete "what is lacking in Christ's afflictions for the sake of his body, that is, the Church" (*Col* 1:24).

In the infancy Gospel, *the proclamation of life*, which comes about in a wondrous way in the birth of the Redeemer, is thus put in sharp contrast with the *threat to life*, a life which embraces the mystery of the Incarnation and of the divine-human reality of Christ in its entirety. The Word was made flesh (cf. *Jn* 1:14): God became man. The Fathers of the Church frequently call attention to this sublime mystery: "God became man, so that we might become gods". This truth of faith is likewise the truth about the human being. It clearly indicates the gravity of all attempts on the life of a child in the womb of its mother. Precisely in this situation we encounter *everything which is diametrically opposed* to "fairest love". If an individual is exclusively concerned with "use", he can reach the point of killing love by killing the fruit of love. For the culture of use, the "blessed fruit of your womb" (*Lk* 1:42) becomes in a certain sense an "accursed fruit".

How can we not recall, in this regard, the aberrations that the so-called *constitutional State* has tolerated in so many countries? The law of God is univocal and categorical with respect to human life. God commands: "You shall not kill" (*Ex* 20:13). *No human lawgiver can therefore assert: it is permissible for you to kill, you have the right to kill, or you should kill.* Tragically, in the history of our century, this has actually occurred when certain political forces have come to power, even by democratic means, and have passed laws contrary to the right to life of every human being, in the name of eugenic, ethnic or other reasons, as unfounded as they are mistaken. A no less serious phenomenon, also because it meets with widespread acquiescence or consensus in public opinion, is that of laws which fail to respect the right to life from the moment of conception. How can one morally accept laws that permit the killing of a human being not yet born, but already alive in the mother's womb? The right to life becomes an exclusive prerogative of adults who even manipulate legislatures in order to carry out their own plans and pursue their own interests.

We are facing an immense threat to life: not only to the life of individuals but also to that of civilization itself. The statement that civilization has become, in some areas, a "civilization of death" is being confirmed in disturbing ways. Was it not a *prophetic event* that the birth of Christ was accompanied by danger to his life? Yes, even the life of the One who is at the same time Son of Man and Son of God was threatened. It was endangered from the very beginning, and only by a miracle did he escape death.

Nevertheless, in the last few decades some consoling signs of a *reawakening of conscience* have appeared: both among intellectuals and in public opinion itself. There is a new and growing sense of respect for life from the first moment of conception, especially among young people. "Pro-life" movements are beginning to spread. This is a leaven of hope for the future of the family and of all humanity.

*"You welcomed me"*

22. Married couples and families of all the world: *the Bridegroom is with you!* This is what the Pope wishes to say to you above all else during this Year which the United Nations and the Church have dedicated to the family. "God so loved the world that he gave his only Son, that whoever believes in him should not perish but have eternal life. For God sent his Son into the world, not to condemn the world, but that the world might be

saved through him" (Jn 3:16-17). "That which is born of the flesh is flesh, and that which is born of the Spirit is spirit.... You must be born anew" (Jn 3:6-7). You must be born "of water and the Spirit" (Jn 3:5). You yourselves, dear fathers and mothers, are the *first witnesses and servants* of this *rebirth* in the Holy Spirit. As you beget children on earth, never forget that *you are also begetting them for God*. God wants their birth in the Holy Spirit. He wants them to be adopted children in the Only-begotten Son, who gives us "power to become children of God" (Jn 1:12). The work of salvation continues in the world and is carried out through the Church. All this is the work of the Son of God, the Divine Bridegroom, who has given to us the Kingdom of his Father and who reminds us, his disciples, that "the Kingdom of God is in the midst of you" (Lk 17:21).

Our faith tells us that Jesus Christ, who "is seated at the right hand of the Father", will come to judge the living and the dead. On the other hand, the Gospel of John assures us that Christ was sent "into the world, not to condemn the world, but that the world might be saved through him" (Jn 3:17). In what then does judgment consist? Christ himself gives the answer: "And this is

the judgment, that the light has come into the world. . . .
But he who does what is true comes into the light, that
it may be clearly seen that his deeds have been wrought
by God" (Jn 3:19, 21). Recently, the Encyclical *Veritatis
Splendor* also reminded us of this. Is Christ then a judge?
*Your own actions will judge you in the light of the truth which
you know.* Fathers and mothers, sons and daughters, will
be judged by their actions. Each one of us will be judged
according to the Commandments, including those we
have discussed in this Letter: the Fourth, Fifth, Sixth
and Ninth Commandments. But ultimately everyone will
be judged *on love*, which is the deepest meaning and
the summing-up of the Commandments. As Saint John
of the Cross wrote: "In the evening of life we shall be
judged on love". Christ, the Redeemer and Bridegroom
of mankind, "was born for this and came into the world
for this, to bear witness to the truth. Everyone who is of
truth hears his voice" (cf. Jn 18:37). Christ will be the
judge, but in the way that he himself indicated in speaking of the Last Judgment (cf. Mt 25:31-46). His will be a
*judgment on love*, a judgment which will definitively confirm the truth that the Bridegroom was with us, without
perhaps our having been aware of it.

# The Bridegroom Is with You

The judge is the *Bridegroom of the Church and of humanity*. This is why he says, in passing his sentence: "Come, O blessed of my Father ... for I was hungry and you gave me food, I was thirsty and you gave me drink, I was a stranger and you welcomed me, I was naked and you clothed me" (Mt 25:34-36). This list could of course be lengthened, and countless other problems relevant to married and family life could be added. There we might very well find statements like: "I was an unborn child, and you welcomed me by letting me be born"; "I was an abandoned child, and you became my family"; "I was an orphan, and you adopted me and raised me as one of your own children". Or again: "You helped mothers filled with uncertainty and exposed to wrongful pressure to welcome their unborn child and let it be born"; and "You helped large families and families in difficulty to look after and educate the children God gave them". We could continue with a long and detailed list, including all those kinds of true moral and human good in which love is expressed. This is *the great harvest* which the Redeemer of the world, to whom the Father has entrusted judgment, will come to reap. It is the *harvest of grace and of good works*, ripened by the breath of the Bridegroom in the Holy Spirit, who is ever at work in the world and in the Church. For all of this, let us give thanks to the Giver of every good gift.

We also know however that according to the Gospel of Matthew the Final Judgment will contain another list, solemn and terrifying: "Depart from me ... for I was hungry and you gave me no food, I was thirsty and you gave me no drink, I was a stranger and you did not welcome me, naked and you did not clothe me" (Mt 25:41-43). To this list also we could add other ways of acting, in which Jesus is present in each case as the *one who has been rejected*. In this way he would identify with the abandoned wife or husband, or with the child conceived and then rejected: "You did not welcome me"! This judgment is also to be found throughout the history of our families; it is to be found throughout the history of our nations and all humanity. Christ's words, "You did not welcome me", also touch social institutions, governments and international organizations.

Pascal wrote that "Jesus will be in agony until the end of the world". The agony of Gethsemane and the agony of Golgotha are *the summit of the revelation of love*. Both scenes reveal the Bridegroom who is with us, who loves us ever anew, and "loves us to the end" (cf. *Jn* 13:1). The love which is in Christ, and which from him flows beyond the limits of individual or family histories, flows beyond the limits of all human history.

At the end of these reflections, dear Brothers and Sisters, in view of what will be proclaimed from various platforms during the Year of the Family, I would like to renew with you the profession of faith which Peter addressed to Christ: "You have the words of eternal life" (*Jn* 6:68). Together let us say: "Your words, O Lord, will not pass away"! (cf. *Mk* 13:31). What then is the Pope's wish for you at the end of this lengthy *meditation on the Year of the Family*? It is his prayer that all of you will be in agreement with these words, which are "spirit and life" (*Jn* 6:63).

*"Strengthened in the inner man"*

23. I bow my knees before the Father, from whom every fatherhood and motherhood is named, "that he may grant you to be strengthened with might through his Spirit in the inner man" (*Eph* 3:16). I willingly return to these words of the Apostle, which I mentioned in the first part of this Letter. In a certain sense they are

pivotal words. *The family, fatherhood and motherhood all go together.* The family is the first human setting in which is formed that "inner man" of which the Apostle speaks. The growth of the inner man in strength and vigour is a gift of the Father and the Son in the Holy Spirit.

The Year of the Family sets before us in the Church an immense task, no different from the task which families face every year and every day. In the context of this Year, however, that task takes on particular meaning and importance. We began the Year of the Family in Nazareth on the *Solemnity of the Holy Family*. Throughout this Year we wish to make our pilgrim way towards that place of grace which has become the *Shrine of the Holy Family* in the history of humanity. We want to make this pilgrimage in order to become aware once again of that heritage of truth about the family which from the beginning has been *a treasure for the Church*. It is a treasure which grows out of the rich tradition of the Old Covenant, is completed in the New and finds its fullest symbolic expression in the mystery of the Holy Family in which the divine Bridegroom brings about the redemption of all families. From there Jesus proclaims the "*gospel of the family*". All generations of Christ's disciples have drawn upon this treasure of truth, beginning with the Apostles, on whose teaching we have so frequently drawn in this Letter.

In our own times this treasure has been examined in depth in the documents of the Second Vatican Council. Perceptive analyses were developed in the many addresses given by Pope Pius XII to newlyweds, in the Encyclical *Humanae Vitae* of Pope Paul VI, in the speeches delivered at the Synod of Bishops on the Family (1980) and in the Apostolic Exhortation *Familiaris Consortio*. I have already spoken of these statements of the Magisterium. If I return to them now, it is in order to emphasize how vast and rich is the *treasure of Christian truth about the family. Written testimonies* alone, however, will not suffice. Much more important are *living testimonies*. As Pope Paul VI observed, "contemporary man listens more willingly to witnesses than to teachers, and if he listens to teachers it is because they are witnesses". In the Church, the treasure of the family has been entrusted first and foremost to witnesses: to those fathers and mothers, sons and daughters who through the family have discovered the path of their human and Christian vocation, the dimension of the "inner man" (*Eph* 3:16) of which the

Apostle speaks, and thus have attained holiness. *The Holy Family is the beginning of countless other holy families.* The Council recalled that holiness is the vocation of all the baptized. In our age, as in the past, there is no lack of witnesses to the "gospel of the family", even if they are not well known or have not been proclaimed saints by the Church. The Year of the Family is the appropriate occasion to bring about an increased awareness of their existence and their great number.

The history of mankind, the history of salvation, passes by way of the family. In these pages I have tried to show how the family is placed at the centre of the great struggle between good and evil, between life and death, between love and all that is opposed to love. To the family is entrusted the task of striving, first and foremost, *to unleash the forces of good,* the source of which is found in Christ the Redeemer of man. *Every family unit needs to make these forces their own so that,* to use a phrase spoken on the occasion of the Millennium of Christianity in Poland, the family will be "*strong with the strength of God*". This is why the present Letter has sought to draw inspiration from the apostolic exhortations found in the writings of Paul (cf. *1 Cor* 7:1-40; *Eph* 5:21-6:9; *Col*

3:25) and the Letters of Peter and John (cf. *1 Pet* 3:1-7; *1 Jn* 2:12-17). Despite the differences in their historical and cultural contexts, how similar are the experiences of Christians and families then and now!

What I offer, then, is *an invitation*: an invitation addressed especially to you, dearly beloved husbands and wives, fathers and mothers, sons and daughters. It is an invitation to all the particular Churches to remain united in the teaching of the apostolic truth. It is addressed to my Brothers in the Episcopate, and to priests, religious families and consecrated persons, to movements and associations of the lay faithful; to our brothers and sisters united by common faith in Jesus Christ, even while not yet sharing the full communion willed by the Saviour; to all who by sharing in the faith of Abraham belong, like us, to the great community of believers in the one God; to those who are the heirs of other spiritual and religious traditions; and to all men and women of good will.

May Christ, who is the same "yesterday and today and for ever" (*Heb* 13:8), be with us as we bow the knee before the Father, from whom all fatherhood and motherhood and every human family is named (cf. *Eph* 3:14-15). In the words of the prayer to the Father which Christ himself taught us, may he once again offer testimony of that love with which he loved us "to the end"! (*Jn* 13:1).

I speak with the power of his truth to all people of our day, so that they will come to appreciate the grandeur of the goods of marriage, family and life; so that they will come to appreciate the great danger which follows when these realities are not respected, or when the supreme values which lie at the foundation of the family and of human dignity are disregarded.

May the Lord Jesus repeat these truths to us *with the power and the wisdom of the Cross*, so that humanity will not yield to the temptation of the "father of lies" (*Jn* 8:44), who constantly seeks to draw people to broad and easy ways, ways apparently smooth and pleasant, but in reality full of snares and dangers. May we always be enabled to follow the One who is "the way, and the truth, and the life" (*Jn* 14:6).

Dear Brothers and Sisters: Let all of this be the task of Christian families and the object of the Church's missionary concern throughout this Year, so rich in singular divine graces. May the Holy Family, icon and model of every human family, help each individual to walk in the spirit of Nazareth. May it help each family unit to grow in understanding of its particular mission in society and the Church by hearing the Word of God, by prayer and by a fraternal sharing of life. May Mary, Mother of "Fairest Love", and Joseph, Guardian of the Redeemer, accompany us all with their constant protection.

With these sentiments I bless every family in the name of the Most Holy Trinity: Father, Son and Holy Spirit.

*Given in Rome, at Saint Peter's, on 2 February, the Feast of the Presentation of the Lord, in the year 1994, the sixteenth of my Pontificate.*

John Paul II

# Study Questions

## Introduction (nos. 1-5)

1. Both the United Nations and the Catholic Church declared 1994 the Year of the Family. Why is the family so important to deserve such attention, even from those who choose to remain single?

2. In 1980, the Synod on the family discussed the "vast and complex experience with regard to the family." St. John Paul II addresses the same theme in this document. The extraordinary Synod on the family in 2014 and the ordinary Synod on the family in 2015 take up the same theme. Has the Church made any progress in her ability to articulate her doctrine on the family? Why does the Church continue to examine the same question?

3. St. John Paul II insists that prayer is essential for successful family life. How can this teaching be made concrete for families, rather than abstract or academic? Are there specific practices that can be recommended for most families?

### I. The Civilization of Love (nos. 6-17)

*The nature of the family [What is the family?]*
*(nos. 6-11)*

1. Why is human procreation different from animal procreation? How is this related to the human vocation?

2. The Bible articulates the principle for the fundamental equality of man and woman. What is that principle, and how does it affect our understanding of all of the sacraments, excluding Holy Orders?

3. The body predisposes man and woman to form a "communion of persons." How does this communion affect the life of spouses together? If the body and soul are intimately united, how should the physical union relate to the spiritual union of the spouses?

4. Why should married couples want children? Is there a danger that people could come to regard children as a commodity?

5. St. John Paul II discussed the concept of the reciprocal "gift of self." What does this concept mean? Does it relate to the indissolubility of marriage? Is the "gift of self" a gift that can be returned or exchanged?

*The responsibility of love (nos. 12-13)*

1. Many people who oppose the Catholic Church's teaching on contraception point to the difficult circumstances into which some children are born. What is the meaning of "responsible parenthood" according to St. John Paul II? How is it different from the "responsibility" offered by contraception? How does the latter endanger the family and the individual?

2. In the English language, the word *love* has many meanings, from the sentimental expression of a greeting card to a profound theological expression ("God is Love"). How then ought we to understand the phrase "civilization of love"?

*The work of love (no. 14)*

1. Why is love "demanding," and how can rediscovering this truth enrich individuals and families?

2. This document describes some children as "orphans of living parents." What does this expression mean? How have these children been affected by particular conceptions of love?

*The school of humanity (nos. 15-17)*

1. The fourth commandment, "Honor your father and your mother," has a reciprocal understanding of "honor your children." What does it mean to honor one's children? Is it right to make these demands of parents? How does this affect our understanding of human rights?

2. Does the Catholic Church place too much confidence in parents to call them the first educators of their children?

3. Given the high rate of divorce for Catholic couples, how might marriage preparation be reconceived as more than a brief course for engaged couples, but instead a substantial inquiry into lifelong happiness?

II. The Bridegroom Is with You (nos. 18-22)

*Marriage, a true sacrament of the new covenant (no. 18)*

1. The relationship between Christ and the Church is described as a nuptial relationship, a marriage. What should be the similarities between the marriage of a man and a woman and the marriage of Christ and the Church?

2. Despite the attacks on marriage, we have been given the sacraments of Baptism, Reconciliation, Confirmation, and the Eucharist. How can these sacraments help us overcome the attacks on marriage?

*The mystery and reality of spousal love (nos. 19-20)*

1. How does a wife respect her husband in a way that does not imply the loss of her own dignity, confirming the reality that she is made in the same image and likeness of God as her husband?

2. Contemporary Western culture has separated radically the human body and the human spirit, to the point at which the two are often understood as wholly separate realities that have nothing to do with each other. Does

this common mentality affect the way Catholics tend to think about the body, sexuality, and marriage? Why and how does this tendency need to be corrected?

3. In no. 17, the pope speaks of a "superficial and false modernity." He later speaks of "modern rationalism" in no. 19. How do these concepts affect the ability to understand what St. Paul calls "the great mystery"? How is it that love, marriage, and family, all of which we can see and identify, are also a mystery?

4. If "fairest love" begins with the self-revelation of the person, and Adam and Eve revealed themselves to each other at creation, does this suggest that we come to know ourselves better as we know others? Can we know ourselves without knowing others?

*Threats to love [Love is threatened] (nos. 21-22)*

1. Can we take courage in the fact that even the Holy Family (Joseph, Mary, and Jesus) suffered attacks from their very beginning as a family? How can this inspire us when we feel attacked either within our own family or from the surrounding culture?

# Study Questions

2. Our actions will judge us in light of the truth that we know. Ultimately, we will be judged on love. How does love shape our actions? What are some concrete examples of how it should shape our families, particularly during times of trial?

*Conclusion (no. 23)*

1. Every family is called to be a holy family. At the same time, there will be suffering, just as Jesus and the Holy Family suffered. How do we understand suffering in the overall context of love?

2. Why should the family be a priority for individuals, families, religions, governments, and other organizations? While other entities support the family, what is uniquely offered by the family? Why is it called the "school of humanity"?

# An Invitation

The book you hold in your hands was published by Sophia Institute for Teachers.

Sophia Institute for Teachers was founded in 2013 as a project of Sophia Institute Press to renew and rebuild Catholic culture through service to Catholic education. With an abiding respect for the role and work of teachers, we strive to provide materials and programs that are at once enlightening to the mind and ennobling to the heart, faithful and complete, as well as useful and practical.

We fulfill our mission by offering Catholic teachers a website on which to share resources and best practices; printed curriculum guides filled with teacher-written, scholar-reviewed, and classroom-tested lesson plans; and professional development programs team-taught by catechetical scholars and master teachers.

If you know a Catholic educator who is seeking enrichment and support in her vocation to educate young people in the Faith, as well as the chance to form friendships with like-minded teachers, please bring our Institute to her attention.

### www.SophiaInstituteforTeachers.org